SELF PSYCHOLOGY AND PSYCHOSIS

SELF PSYCHOLOGY AND PSYCHOSIS
The Development of the Self during Intensive Psychotherapy of Schizophrenia and Other Psychoses

*David Garfield
and Ira Steinman*

KARNAC

First published in 2015 by
Karnac Books Ltd
118 Finchley Road
London NW3 5HT

Copyright © 2015 by David Garfield and Ira Steinman

The rights of David Garfield and Ira Steinman to be identified as the authors of this work has been asserted in accordance with §§ 77 and 78 of the Copyright Design and Patents Act 1988.

All rights reserved. No part of this publication may be reproduced, stored in a retrieval system, or transmitted, in any form or by any means, electronic, mechanical, photocopying, recording, or otherwise, without the prior written permission of the publisher.

We are indebted to Karnac Books for allowing the republication of material previously published in *Treating the "Untreatable": Healing in the Realms of Madness* by I. M. Steinman, 2009, London: Karnac.

British Library Cataloguing in Publication Data

A C.I.P. for this book is available from the British Library

ISBN-13: 978-1-78220-228-8

Typeset by V Publishing Solutions Pvt Ltd., Chennai, India

Printed in Great Britain

www.karnacbooks.com

SONNET X

When to the sessions of sweet silent thought
I summon up remembrance of things past,
I sigh the lack of many a thing I sought,
And with old woes new wail my dear time's waste:
Then can I drown an eye, unused to flow,
For precious friends hid in death's dateless night,
And weep afresh love's long since cancelled woe,
And moan the expense of many a vanished sight:
Then can I grieve at grievances foregone,
And heavily from woe to woe tell o'er
The sad account of fore-bemoaned moan,
Which I new pay as if not paid before.
But if the while I think on thee, dear friend,
All losses are restor'd and sorrows end.

—*William Shakespeare*

CONTENTS

ACKNOWLEDGEMENTS	ix
ABOUT THE AUTHORS	xi
PREFACE Coming to self psychology	xiii
INTRODUCTION Self psychology and psychosis	xxiii
PRELUDE AND ENTRE Cross modal attunement and revitalization of the self	xxxi

PART I: MIRRORING

CHAPTER ONE The opening phase—the case of Judith	3

CHAPTER TWO
Judith—the middle phase   23

CHAPTER THREE
Repair of the self—Judith   47

CHAPTER FOUR
The infrastructure of the vertical split   59

PART II: IDEALIZING

CHAPTER FIVE
Rachel—in need of an internal safe haven   81

CHAPTER SIX
Three rats and the extraterrestrial   97

PART III: ALIKENESS (TWINSHIP)

CHAPTER SEVEN
Jonathan and the twinship transference   109

CHAPTER EIGHT
Selfobjects in psychosis—the twinship compensation   129

CHAPTER NINE
The widening scope of psychoanalysis:
   self psychology and psychosis   147

REFERENCES   151

INDEX   157

ACKNOWLEDGEMENTS

David Garfield

In memory of Marian Tolpin, Paul Tolpin, and Leston Havens—their unique blend of inspiration and loving support will never be forgotten.

I am sustained and encouraged by my wife, Bonnie, my brother Rob and sister, Deborah, my daughter, Jenny and my son, Jacob.

Jack and Madeline Neems, Jake Kriger, Mike and Laurie Jacker, Michael Seidenberg and LeiAnn Marshall, Howard Resnick and Nutan Vaidya are the pillars of what holds me up on a day-to-day basis.

Ira Steinman

To my dear wife Alice, from whom I have learned nearly everything.

ABOUT THE AUTHORS

David Garfield is Professor, Associate Chair, and Director of Residency Training in the Department of Psychiatry and Behavioral Sciences at Rosalind Franklin University of Medicine and Science, Chicago Medical School. He is also faculty at the Insitute for Psychoanalysis, Chicago.

Ira Steinman practices in-depth psychiatry in San Francisco, focusing on the intensive psychotherapy of severely disturbed people. His early training included work with R. D. Laing, residency with Bob Wallerstein at Mount Zion, and a stint at the National Academy of Sciences evaluating the efficacy of all psychiatric medications. He is the author of *Treating the "Untreatable": Healing in the Realms of Madness* (Karnac, 2009).

PREFACE

Coming to self psychology

David Garfield

I was standing in the lobby of Harvard's Massachusetts Mental Health Center in 1981 when an energetic social worker approached me and asked, "Do you have a copy of Kohut's book *Analysis of the Self*?" I had seen it and had glanced through it but it was so incredibly dense that I had decided not to buy it. I said, "No, I don't," and she bounded off looking elsewhere for it as she had just joined a small study group of faculty who were reading it. It was my second year of residency. I had, however, been a pretty avid reader and had been completely hooked on working with psychotic patients from a modified psychoanalytic viewpoint that focused on affect. That focus was the gift of my professional grandfather, Elvin Semrad, whom I had never met. He had died a few years prior to my arrival and the hospital was slowly coming out of its mourning process. In the meantime, when I wasn't with patients, I immersed myself in the Center's library, reading Semrad's published and unpublished writings and learning from his closest students—Tom Gutheil, Doris Benaron, Max Day and Leston Havens. Over several decades, Semrad had taught dozens of Boston area analysts and left an indelible mark on them and I wanted to absorb all of it.

I came to the psychotherapy of psychosis honestly, having been an English major at Haverford College where I wrote my honors thesis on William Butler Yeats and his search for the self. It left me convinced that no corner of human experience should be ignored and in fact, every corner of human experience should be embraced. I lucked out after college by being admitted to the University of California, San Francisco Medical School where alongside a fantastic traditional medical education, the city's milieu exposed me to Rolfing, diagnosis of illness by iridology, foot reflexology, acupuncture, astrology, shamanism, and Carlos Castenada—you name it, San Francisco had it. Alongside medicine, I started my more serious studies in Tai Chi Chuan while I was there. I was like a kid in an intellectual candy store whose marquee read, "come here to learn about becoming a healer." I thrived in my third year psychiatry clerkship at Mount Zion (I didn't know Ira then) where I was introduced to Margaret Mahler's work and I took an independent study on Freud's *Interpretation of Dreams* and I threw myself into a fourth year elective on inpatient psychiatry with Renee Binder. I was fortunate to be accepted to Harvard's Massachussets Mental Health Center for psychiatry residency, so I was going. I stopped home for a year of internal medicine in Chicago at Cook County Hospital to prove to myself that I was a real doctor and so I could expose myself to their trauma unit and those "extremes of human life."

Once I had my feet planted in Boston and through my pursuit of Semrad, I came to understand that the heart of his affect centered work lay in the empathic process—prelude to Kohut. It was "experience-near." Trying to bring a bit of San Francsico to Boston, I started "FAPP" in my residency cohort—the Forum for the Advancement of the Psychotherapy of Psychosis, consisting of a motley group of residents and psychology interns. We invited Sullivanians, Jungians, object relations folks and others to speak to us at pizza dinners we organized at our apartments. It was as electric as it was eclectic. Kohut was only then starting to take hold in Boston. Self psychology had not yet really taken hold outside of Chicago.

During my final year of training in Boston, I went to Yale to visit my old childhood friend, Richard Lane—(now an affect neuroimaging professor/researcher at the U of Arizona) to attend a psychotherapy of psychosis symposium sponsored by Stephen Fleck and Ted Lidz. I started a wonderful relationship with ISPS (now, the International Society for the Psychological and Social Approaches to Psychosis) and found a professional home for myself with this incredibly dedicated and growing group of psychiatrists, psychologists, and social workers from around the world who engage in all sorts of creative ways with seriously mentally ill people. This is how Ira and I met.

After Boston, I eventually returned home to Chicago as a residency director at Chicago Medical School and was immediately drawn to Dr. Marian Tolpin, one of Kohut's main students. I trained in psychoanalysis at the Chicago Institute and found my connection between Semrad and Kohut ... first in *Unbearable Affect—A Guide to Psychotherapy of Psychosis* and now, in this volume that Ira and I have been working on for the last several years—*Self Psychology and Psychosis*.

Ira Steinman

This book grew out of a symposium I organized at ISPS (The International Society for the Psychological and Social Approaches to Psychosis) in Madrid in 2006, where I presented a number of successfully treated cases demonstrating the value of an intensive psychotherapy of schizophrenia. David Garfield, one of the discussants, did such a stellar job that we decided to put our heads together and collaborate on this book. As David and I thought about our book, it became clear that this would be a book about not only the psychotherapy of schizophrenia, but about the all important development of the self during the intensive psychotherapy of schizophrenia.

I'd never been a Kohutian. In fact, until David told me that I was an intuitive self psychotherapist, I hadn't thought too much about the subject of self psychology, assuming that it was a given that we all had a sense of self. I had always seen people as people with many different aspects, though often beset by myriad difficulties, including the belief in the reality of hallucinations and delusions, if overtly psychotic, or the belief in many different beings existing in them if they were somewhere on the dissociative spectrum of disorders. So, I began to think about how I had begun and quickly practiced a method of treatment that seemed so self psychological.

As I thought about my interest in psychosis, I remembered the obvious. Not only was schizophrenia fascinating, but I had very close contact with it as a child. I had an arch-enemy, the son of a prominent family in the small town in which I grew up. He and I would battle for a number of years, with large gangs of his allies fighting against my always smaller, hopefully cagier, forces. Eventually, our nearly decade long intermittent battle ended when he burned his garage down with flaming arrows and was sent off to boarding school; he had been planning a flaming arrow attack on my house and was practicing.

He was not the psychotic one, though; he was just an angry, somewhat needy and psychopathic kid. The schizophrenic one was his mother, who was hospitalized with post-partum psychosis, from the age of three to five, after the birth of another child. When she came home, she was an ethereal, spiritual person, always willing to talk with me—and anyone else who showed an interest—about her pursuit of God. For the next fifteen years, I found her always of interest, strange and perplexing. Even as a boy, I wondered what made her tick.

I always read a lot growing up, exploring character and development as portrayed through novelists' eyes and words. At Brown, I turned to Honors English as a Major, continuing the study and discussion of other's lives. It was much fun. But, being the child of an immigrant, I had work to do and tired of the ease of college. I got in to medical school at nineteen and left with no college degree.

I was not particularly fond of medical school, either. This was lucky, for it threw me back into myself, into a long period of self-observation of who I was and how I had gotten here. This introspective time put me in contact with the dynamic forces within me, and an awareness of how I had become who I was. In short, it was an exploration of my own self and self-development.

At Albert Einstein, with its Freudian oriented department of psychiatry, we were encouraged to spend a great deal of time getting to know our schizophrenic patients in depth. While on the wards, I did evaluations lasting up to two months of severely psychotic people, of manic depressives, of anorexia nervosa—so called at the time—of paranoid schizophrenia. It was an argumentative department, with existentialists and Jungians as well as rather doctrinaire Freudians. Our classroom discussions whet my appetite for more; our psychiatric library was ecumenical as was our faculty. Milt Rosenbaum headed the psychiatry department and Norm Reider, Ed Hornick, and Wil Tanenbaum emphasized the various aspects of Freudian thought, while John Thompson, an English Jungian, provided an elegant philosophical and literary counterpoint and Iz Zwerling provided a community mental health oriented view.

I quickly saw patients as whole people, not just raging battle grounds for id and super-ego issues, projecting this or hallucinating that. I thought of them as others very much like me, but suffering various conflicts and psychologically induced difficulties that—depending on the age of onset and environmental and often traumatic circumstances—had led them into the morass of schizophrenic and delusional disorders. It was the interplay of so many forces—internal psychological forces such as yearnings and super-ego conflicts, guilt and retreat from painful circumstances—that was a fascinating study. Exploring and making sense of such diverse phenomena as the symbolic meaning of a hallucination, its origin in affect laden circumstances and its possible meaning to the patient were the grist of the psychotherapeutic mill.

One day, John Rosen (1953) gave Grand Rounds and made numerous interpretations and clarifications to a schizophrenic patient in front of a large audience. It was interesting to watch. What he said to the patient made a lot of sense to the group, and even to the patient. Did it last, though? Most of us doubted that such a one shot approach would hold for long. That's where an ongoing psychodynamic psychotherapy helping the patient deal with the meaning to him of hallucinations and delusions would come into play.

In reading about schizophrenia, I came across a book by Ronnie Laing, *The Divided Self* (1962). It was fascinating, trying to make schizophrenia comprehensible within the context of a person's life, experiences and interactions with family members. Feeling alienated, the schizoid or schizophrenic person develops a false self, which often breaks down in a schizophrenic crisis. Intrigued, I read Laing's *The Self and Others*, (1961) which focuses on the relations between people and interactions that can lead to breakdown and psychosis both in clinical cases and in Dostoevsky's *Crime and Punishment*. Liking what I read and wanting to travel, I contacted him and convinced him and the medical school to let me spend the better part of the last year of medical school studying schizophrenia with him and his colleagues in London.

Days were spent either in Laing's office discussing cases and readings with him and Aaron Esterson (1964), who had a definite vision of family dynamics being a major part of the development of schizophrenia, or at Shenley Hospital in Dunstable north of London, where I spent time in the anti-hospital Villa 21 with Laing's colleague David Cooper (1964). For a period of time, I lived on the unit with the psychotic people there, just another person talking, hanging out and trying to fathom what might have made each of them so disturbed. One fellow about my age—twenty-three at the time—had been hospitalized in Villa 21 with the terrifying and phobic certainty that nuclear destruction was imminent. He believed he and England would be annihilated at any moment. Gradually, as we talked—with no antipsychotic medications—he came to realize that his family situation, and his anger at it, fueled his belief in nuclear Armageddon. Nuclear destruction from the outside symbolized both his father's rage and his pent up fury at the way he, his siblings and mother had been treated by his abusive father. Understanding his metaphor, his terror began to abate.

Kingsley Hall (Barnes & Berke, 1991) was just beginning, so I spent a while there as it started. Here too, the goal was to help psychotic people understand their difficulties and make sense of previously incomprehensible hallucinations, delusions, and psychotic phenomena via a regressive therapy without medication. Laing and I would talk about this as a treatment option; there were a number of nights when he wished he could take someone to a hospital or use medications, but the group persevered in their determination to try to heal psychosis through helping the patient understand his or her internal workings that had led to the schizophrenic break. Of course, Laing, his colleagues and the Philadelphia association all discussed psychiatric theory, issues and cases, as well as philosophy, religions and cultural questing. After all, it was 1964 and 1965 and intellectual ferment and questioning were beginning to sweep the US and Europe. It was a heady experience for a young trainee.

I interned in Berkeley and followed my developing interest in the psychotherapy of psychosis. I immersed myself for months in the psychiatric wards, working with and talking to many very disturbed patients. Depending on the clinician, I could spend as long as I wanted trying to understand how these people had gotten into their psychotic predicaments. Again, psychosis remained fascinating for me. I also spent a period of time during that internship year exploring gestalt psychology approaches to schizophrenia and bi-polar disorder (Perls, 1941).

Due to the Vietnam War, I ended up in Washington DC in the Public Health Service where I worked with Danny Freedman (1966) as the executive secretary for the National Academy of Sciences Panel (1969) evaluating the efficacy of all psychiatric drugs. During these two years of Public Heath Service, I was able to spend time at weekly Wednesday afternoon seminars at Chestnut Lodge, hearing some of the greats of psychiatry: Otto Will, Harold Searles (1965), Milton Hendlich (Stern et al., 1995), Jarl Dyrud (1975), Dexter Bullard (1939), and Ping-Nie Pao (1979) to name a few, present their case material and lead lively and engaging discussions on the benefit of an in-depth intensive psychodynamic psychotherapy in schizophrenics and other severely disturbed and hospitalized patients. Again, it was a time of learning.

What was I learning? That there was a whole person who needed to be treated. It was not a simple matter of id or ego or super-ego. These were nomenclature, attempts to try to describe what a person was going through, how he had developed and the forces that played such a large part in his development. To me, the self was supraordinate.

Chestnut Lodge had been heavily influenced by Harry Stack Sullivan and his interpersonal psychiatry. Sullivan felt that relationships were of utmost importance in the development of the individual. Through an exploration of a person's significant relationships, we could understand both the "self system" and personality traits as he or she developed. In addition, we could fathom the "security operations" developed in childhood to ward off anxiety and perceived threats to well-being and self-esteem. Sullivan felt that the important factors were interactional, not intrapsychic (1953).

His views influenced a generation of followers ranging from Frieda Fromm-Reichmann (1950) to Otto Will (1961). Whereas Sullivan emphasized the interpersonal and Freud the intrapsychic, Fromm-Reichmann tried to meld the two seemingly divergent viewpoints, in order that we could truly understand the person in his or her totality, both intrapsychic and interpersonal. Otto Will carried on Fromm-Reichmann's views on the benefits of intensive psychotherapy with psychosis, as did the other practitioners and researchers at the Chestnut Lodge conferences.

So, the importance of the self, its interactions with others and internal psychodynamics were stressed at both Chestnut Lodge and during my sojourn in England with Laing.

I moved back to San Francisco for my residency at Mount Zion Hospital. This was one of the foremost psychodynamic psychotherapy programs in the country at the time, under the direction of Bob Wallerstein (1958 with Eckstein; 1986) and the tutelage of Ed Weinshel. The program focused on dynamic psychotherapy of neurotic and character disordered people, but also gave us a long stint of doing dynamic psychotherapy while on the inpatient unit.

Even though the staff at Mount Zion had a primarily Freudian orientation, it was psychodynamic to the core, including teachings from other schools, such as the American and English Object Relations Schools. Melanie Klein's paranoid and depressive positions in infancy, Bowlby's attachment theory, Kernberg's interest in drive theory interacting with early environmental experiences, Balint's primitive relatedness of infancy and its vicissitudes, Mahler's phases of development culminating in separation/individuation and rapprochement and Winnicott's concepts of the good-enough Mother and a decent holding environment for healthy development were notions with which we all became familiar. It was very clear that people developed and ran into trouble not just for intrapsychic reasons, but also due to difficulties in their most important early relationships. But nowhere during my training at Mount Zion, did I hear of the self.

I had worked with Sid Jourard, author of *The Transparent Self* in London in 1964 and 1965. We all had read Erving Goffman's *The Presentation of Self in Everyday Life*. Buddhist thought was filled with notions of the self and the analysis of attachment to the self. Hindu thought seemed built upon, Atman and Brahman, the little self and the great self pervading creation. I had spent months during my time at the National Academy poring over Sartre's *L'Etant et le Neant, Being and Nothingness* in which he described the development of the self, the "for itself" and the "in itself" from an existentialist perspective. Winnicott talked of the true self and the false self; existentialists wrote of authentic and inauthentic behavior and ways of being, of the inauthentic and authentic self. Jung spoke of the self as an archetype of an individuated person, unifying both conscious and unconscious mind. Maslow's term self-actualization had made it into mainstream thought.

During residency, however, people were conceptualized differently. Intrapsychic forces played the major role, but interpersonal issues were crucial in the development of conflicts around issues like neediness and anger and sexuality. Doctrinaire Freudians stressed oedipal issues; more eclectic types talked of the importance of pre-oedipal issues, especially in the development and treatment of the severely disturbed. The emphasis was on the development of the person, with little or no thought or talk of the self; environmental forces and intrapsychic issues and conflicts were paramount.

In short, there was a person with a (hopefully) developing sense of self. But, in training, we didn't really talk of the self. We talked of a person, with conflicts and psychological issues, conflicts rooted in early experience. Emphasis on the oedipal was waning for some of us.

I pressed on with an interest in the pre-oedipal, with my patient's earliest experiences in their lives, ideas that fit in perfectly with the English object relation school of Winnicott, Fairbairn, and Guntrip. Fairbairn emphasized the importance not of instincts and drives, but of early relationships and their influence on the development of a positive sense of self.

Harry Guntrip, in his *Schizoid Phenomena, Object Relations and the Self*, speaks not only theoretically, but practically, describing the importance of reaching what he termed "the lost heart of the self" the fearful, vulnerable, deepest level of another's being (Guntrip, 1969, p. 87). He emphasized the necessity of sitting with that lost heart, dealing with all the transference and countertransference issues that might develop and being there as an open person to gradually help that inchoate self experience contact and find warmth in the therapeutic relationship. Such contact and movement, which is imperceptible at first, gradually leads to growth and development.

One extremely important factor in my work with very disturbed people is the importance of understanding a patient's symbolism, as contained in hallucinations and delusions. A good working alliance aids in helping the person make sense of confusion and distortions of reality. The closer one gets to the "lost heart of the self" the easier it is to make sense of previously indecipherable and upsetting material. In the course of such work, the patient understands that she is the creator of whatever bizarre phenomena afflict her, and that hallucinations and delusions can be understood. Gradually, hallucinations and delusions are seen to be an amplification of one's own self, rather like symbolic stereo for one's ideas, hopes and fears.

Speaking schizophrenese, making sense of psychotic productions, is the glue that makes therapy with the most disturbed work. To me, this is one of the more important aspects of the psychotherapy of schizophrenia. As one understands a patient's metaphor and symbolism encased in delusions or hallucinations, a beach-head of rationality gets established. From this burgeoning spot, it is possible to understand the meaning and import of hallucinations and delusions, gradually lessening the powerful affects, identifications, and internal constructs that have kept patients in thrall to their demons.

The cases set out in this book will show how simple it is to read another's symbolism and how meaningful and rewarding it is to understand what is meant by a vision, a hallucination, or a delusion.

Once understood as a possible meaning, as Norm Reider and Edward Glover's inexact interpretation, there is both a framework with which to understand and even more importantly, a sense from the patient that they can be understood, that there is someone else there willing to make sense of the previously indecipherable. With that halting first understanding, there is the reward of more and more material presented to be understood, and with each understanding, there is a deeper more meaningful movement to the core of the person who has been so objectified.

How can one ever get to the "lost heart of the self" via excessive use of antipsychotic medication? To me, such a practice is both objectifying of the patient, turning him into an "it" or "the other," and ineffectual.

If, however, one attempts to make sense of a patient's utterances and thoughts, one may be amply rewarded with healing and change, and—at times—a cure of a previously incomprehensible and seemingly intractable schizophrenic condition. Such successful work is described in my *Treating the "Untreatable": Healing in the Realms of Madness* (2009). But to do this, via an intensive psychotherapy, one needs to make sense of a patient's productions, however bizarre they may seem to be, to learn to speak their language, the inchoate and often unknown language they are speaking. One must learn schizophrenese, to speak the language of symbols and the preconscious and unconscious. Only then, do we get to the "lost heart of the self," the place, the state, the flux of intersubjective relatedness that is the prerequisite for change and healing.

INTRODUCTION

Self psychology and psychosis

Nowhere do psychoanalysts and psychotherapists of all persuasions more clearly find distortions of the self than those they encounter who are caught in the throes of psychosis. As hallucinations, delusions and thought disorder take hold, patients struggle mightily to regain their footing. Here, a positive coloring of the self, a temporal continuity within the self and a cohesiveness of the self (Stolorow & Lachmann, 1980) are frequently lost or stand in immediate danger of dissolution. Where could we find a better place for an understanding of the essence of self than in these x-rays of a shattered mind?

Throughout the history of psychoanalysis, references to and understandings of the self are almost too numerous to count (Ellenberger, 1970; Westen, 1992; Kohut, 1971). Yet, what makes psychoanalytic self psychology so compelling as a framework for understanding psychosis is how it links together the early recognition of narcissistic impairment in these disorders to the "experience-near" focus which is the hallmark of self psychology. Freud (1914), early on, had eschewed the wisdom of using psychoanalysis as a vehicle for cure in the "narcissistic neuroses" (psychoses) and even Kohut took years before he embraced the idea that psychoanalysis could have a salutary effect on psychosis. Here he is, musing on this very question with candidates at the Chicago Institute for Psychoanalysis on 14 March 1975. At this particular Institute lecture, the candidate was asking about the relationship between paranoid psychosis and unconscious homosexuality vis a vis Freud's Schreber case. Let's listen in …

> So, to return to your question, when we speak of homosexuality in the initial stages of paranoia, it is not that the paranoia has been erected as a defense against this horrible homosexuality from which the patient then must escape because it is so shameful and implies castration. I don't think it's that at all. I think that the homosexuality is the edge of the cliff to which one wants desperately to hang on to keep from slipping further over the edge. But that last clutching grasp, that last try, does not hold and the organized self breaks into pieces at the bottom of the cliff. The disintegration takes place completely, and then primitive, disruptive aspects of the disorganized self are incongruently pressed together in an attempt to rebuild the self again … normal self-confidence become bizarrely overgrown, isolated in remote, detached, psychotic grandiosity; primitive merger experiences, instead of being empathic and friendly as they ought to be felt, are psychotically rebuilt as if they were influencing forces from others, usually with a hostile non empathic intent. (Tolpin & Tolpin, 1996, p. 283)

Kohut brings us back to the Humpty Dumpty analogy, but, in it, notice the reference to "falling" as opposed to being "uplifted." We will return to this often, later in the book. Perhaps most importantly for our project, is Kohut's last comment in this section:

> A refined understanding of these is what I think will give us access, empathic access, to psychosis. If you really can achieve empathic access to psychosis, psychosis in one sense has ceased to exist. (Tolphin & Tolphin, 1996, p. 283)

A refined empathic access? Earlier in 1959, Kohut steered modern psychoanalysis toward a new way of understanding patients in his groundbreaking article, "Introspection, empathy and psychoanalysis."

Free association, the lynchpin of understanding what happens in the mind of the patient had reigned supreme as the primary access route to what is going on "in depth." Kohut suggested instead that through "vicarious introspection" the analyst must look inside and find "a taste" of what the patient is experiencing. By "accessing" experiences of a similar affective tone, an attunement can be established affording clinicians entre to this more refined understanding. It is not that free association is tossed out, but rather, its role in collecting information about the patient is subordinated to that of empathy. The last fifty years has seen a blossoming of ideas and methods relating to empathic attunement to psychosis which we will further explicate in the pages ahead.

Key ideas

In this volume, we invite the reader to join us, in session, with patients struggling with psychosis. These are real life experiences and in them, one will find the ideas and tools of psychoanalytic self psychology at work.

1. It is almost always, in the "forward edge" (Tolpin, 2002) tendrils of health, reaching out and embraced, that the reader will witness the establishment of a workable analytic relationship.
2. It is in the understanding and discussion of the fears of retraumatization (Bacal, 1985, p. 218), that once disconfirmed, the reader will see the birth of a self reflective capacity emerge. Viewing defense mechanisms as "fears of being retraumatized," brings an entirely different attitude to the "analysis of defense" as an important way of thinking in the opening phase of treatment.
3. The centrality of affect in the body/mind (Garfield, 2009) is a hallmark of the clinician's directed efforts in working with patient's who are reconstituting. Perceptual distortion manifest in hallucination and the decomposition and/or fixation of unbearable sensory/affective experience in delusion and the impact of hopelessness on the disconnection of communication from intent in thought disorder all seek their reintegration via a therapeutic re-embodiment of the mind in the psychoanalytic process.

Reflecting on Kohut's seminar's on Freud, Allen Siegel (1996) noted: "Kohut has an overriding concern about the psyche's capacity to experience intense affects and remain intact. He is

sensitive to the tendency of the psyche to fracture under the burden of unmanageable affects."
4. Daniel Stern's (1985, 2004, 2010) notions about vitality affects/forms of vitality and their intrinsic position at the intersection of body and mind are new tools in the quest for re-establishing cohesion. Intrapsychic coherence is the objective.
5. An empathic grasp of the patient lends a hand to help keep the patient from falling further into a pit or off the cliff and an in-depth understanding of the patient "stands under" the patient allowing for the possibility of the patient gaining some footing. Finding one's balance mitigates against the forces of becoming "unbalanced." Note the physicality of the metaphors we choose in this explication. They are body based. A positive affective coloring is the goal (Stolorow & Lachmann, 1980).
6. Opening channels between the past and the present and hopes for the future is the day to day work of all psychoanalysts, yet, in the psychoanalytic self psychology of psychosis, one of its primary intentions is to help restore a lost sense of temporal continuity.
7. Moving from nascent to durable mirroring, idealizing and twinship selfobject transferences to the analyst signal the ongoing process of reintegration and the vehicle for reviving the Tolpin "tendril's of development" that had become arrested and lost to the past.
8. Self psychology's understanding of rage and destructiveness is another key concept that enhances work with psychotic patients. As Siegel notes (1996), for Kohut, "destructiveness is not the expression of a primary drive. Destructiveness, instead, is the product of a disintegrating self. Destructive rage is always motivated by an injury" (Siegel, 1996, p. 115). Knowing that narcissistic rage can be a breakdown of assertiveness, caused by narcissistic injury, a result of the analyst's empathic miss or failure or as a product of a disintegrating self all help to steer the clinician in the direction of helping the patient "regroup." These concepts lead to better "empathic access."
9. Although Freud (1914) hinted that narcissism had its own developmental trajectory in his paper "On Narcissism," this proposition had to wait until Kohut's (1966) "Forms and Transformations of Narcissism" to more fully take shape. Freud's earlier work took early "self love" that the infant exhibited and saw it evolve into his concept of the "ego ideal." Side by side with the

well-known developmental pathway for object libido through its oral, anal, phallic, oedipal and further stages, the "self preservative instincts" or the "ego libido" or the "ego instincts" underwent their own unconscious developmental evolution into more mature configurations.

What is of particular interest in this regard is Kohut's immediate reference to psychosis at the start of his first monograph on self psychology, *Analysis of the Self* (1971). Diagram One (p. 9), reproduced below, is instrumental in seeing that Kohut was tuned into psychotic psychopathology from the onset of his development of self psychology.

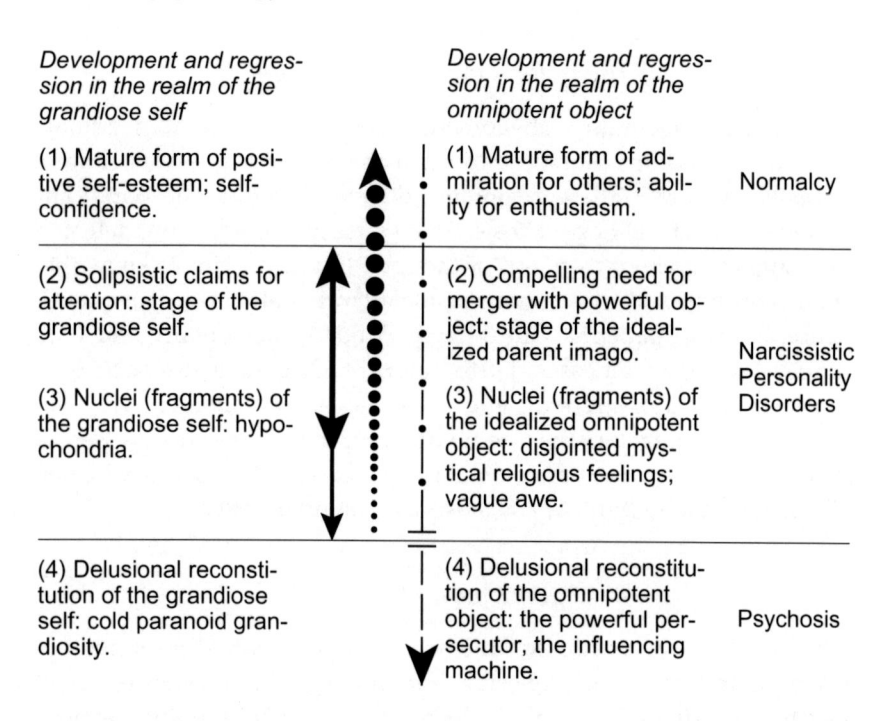

Development and regression in the realm of the grandiose self	*Development and regression in the realm of the omnipotent object*	
(1) Mature form of positive self-esteem; self-confidence.	(1) Mature form of admiration for others; ability for enthusiasm.	Normalcy
(2) Solipsistic claims for attention: stage of the grandiose self. (3) Nuclei (fragments) of the grandiose self: hypochondria.	(2) Compelling need for merger with powerful object: stage of the idealized parent imago. (3) Nuclei (fragments) of the idealized omnipotent object: disjointed mystical religious feelings; vague awe.	Narcissistic Personality Disorders
(4) Delusional reconstitution of the grandiose self: cold paranoid grandiosity.	(4) Delusional reconstitution of the omnipotent object: the powerful persecutor, the influencing machine.	Psychosis

10. The "vertical split" is an important component of self psychology in terms of understanding psychopathology. Here, the unmodified "grandiose" self is excluded from the area of the realistic sector of the mind through the use of disavowal. Another of Kohut's early students and collaborators, Arnold Goldberg, has explored this phenomena extensively and it has, as we will show, real relevance for those with psychotic disorders.

11. It is through the recurrence of psychotic symptomatology that the reader will see the opportunity (as well as danger) for a strengthening process of empathic disruption and repair (Wolf, 1988). Through our case examples, the microstructures and micro processes of psychoanalytic self psychology will reveal themselves as vital elements of the therapeutic armementarium.
12. Another key idea in the mechanism of therapeutic action and harbinger of cure is the that of "enlistment" (Wolf, 1988). This is an additional core idea in self psychology wherein the patient has developed a capacity to recruit individuals or activities that serve as ongoing selfobject experiences.

The heterogeneity of psychosis

Psychosis is not a unitary phenomena. There are two important adjunctive understandings that are important in guiding the re-annealing of patients who are in these disorganized states of mind. The symptoms that evoke the label of psychosis are invariably hallucination, delusion or disorganized behavior and/or thought. It is important to know that these symptoms of dissolution, or maladaptive attempts at reorganization occur in patients with different kinds of personality and with different kinds of illnesses. Furthermore, each patient has their own particular blend of strengths and weaknesses, vulnerability, and resiliency. These are factors that are no different than those encountered in working with neurotic patients but these facts are often obscured when clinicians begin to think of psychosis as a singular entity.

Organization of the book

After an "Entre and prelude," the book is divided into three parts representing the three main cohering "forward edge" transferences of self psychology—the mirroring, idealizing, and twinship selfobject experiences. The first three chapters take the reader through Ira Steinman's ten-year treatment of Judith. Here the basic tenets of self psychology in the opening, middle and closing phases of treatment are explicated. The psychopathology of psychosis is discussed in Judith's treatment in terms of developmental arrest due to deficit and the role of the vertical split in understanding additional features of psychopathology of psychosis is elaborated in Chapter Five, through two of Dr. Garfield's cases.

Part II, Idealizing, continues with Dr. Steinman's treatment of Rachel and illustrates the gradual establishment of an idealizing selfobject transference and its role in helping her regain her footing as she emerges from her psychosis. A shorter case of Dr. Steinman's, "Three rats and the extraterrestrial" follows, also pointing to how a deep, idealizing experience strengthens and transforms a self organized by defensive compensatory delusions.

Part III covers the twinship or "alikeness" selfobject pathway beginning with the mysterious case of Jonathan. Jonathan was a long term treatment in which Dr. Steinman's in depth understanding of Jonathan's devastating loss of himself to meditative practices lay the groundwork for an empathic rescue from a near tragic outcome. Our last chapter in Part III is actually a reprint of an article written by Dr. Garfield and the late, Dr. Marion Tolpin, reprinted with permission from the *American Journal of Psychotherapy*, illustrating through three cases, a fascinating phenomena of "shared body parts" in psychosis as a restorative twinship experience.

PRELUDE AND ENTRE

Cross modal attunement and revitalization of the self

Cross modal attunement: gateway to selfobject experience

At the heart of the many cases explicated in this volume is a fundamental focus on rekindling arrested development of primary psychological needs. When we talk about "deficit" this is that to which we are referring. Although Kohut (1971, 1977, 1984) established the mirroring, idealizing, and twinship selfobject experiences as the avenues though which self structure takes on durability and vitality, we would like to explore an aspect of analytic carpentry that Daniel Stern (1985, 2010) has referred to as "cross modal attunement." In 2001, Garfield brought cross modal attunement into the analytic armamentarium with regard to the coalescence of self in psychosis. As a "gateway" to the basic selfobject avenues—mirroring, idealizing, and twinship, cross modal attunement works, at an interactional level, to "stitch and weave" together the psychic underlay of the self. In 2009, Garfield illustrated this process.

Let's listen into how the fictional psychiatry resident Tony Potter (Garfield, 2009) interacts and muses with his inpatient Iris who suffers with bipolar affective disorder with psychosis. Iris was supposed to receive a visit from her mother.

Fighting with Iris

As he was mulling over Freud's comments on the body ego being the first ego, it occurred to him that Iris had just taken a swing at him and missed his face by an inch. Startled, he saw her smile.

"Potter, are you listening to me?" Iris demanded. She was incredibly agitated. Staff had her on "one to one" because she had pushed one of them while discussing her mother coming for a visit.

Tony: you wanna fight? he teased.

Iris smiles again. Somehow his playfulness settled her down ....

There was something about her taking a swing physically and his taking a swing verbally, yet lovingly, that was a "match." ... Tony began to sense that connection to important "others" and this underlying kinetic "current" of emotion may be related.

In anticipation of her mother's visit, Iris notes:

"OK. She drives me crazy ... but she knows me well, knows a lot about me ... oh, I don't know what I'm saying but she's my mother and she should be allowed to see me."

Dr. Potter responded: Look Iris, the staff are just trying to look out for you. You had this huge blow-out with your mother and things are just starting to settle down. They just don't want her upsetting you again. I can appreciate that she's one of the few people you feel really close to—even if she does aggravate you, so let me see what I can do—maybe for a short visit with a staff referee—what do you think?

Iris: OK, Dr. P., OK, we'll have a referee ... put up your mitts ... she gleefully put her hands into a boxer's stance ...

Potter responds: The only mitts I'm getting are to keep these paws from freezing out there ... (Garfield, 2009, p. 60)

The primacy of movement

In a deep understanding of the "primacy of movement," Maxine Sheets-Johnstone (1998) presents a tour de force examination of the primary role of movement in language, culture, thought and consciousness. If affect, as we posit, is the "circulatory system of the self," it begs the question "is there an infrastructure of the selfobject experience that involves movement in some fashion?" As we explicate later, Kohut's (1984) and Tolpin's (2002) ideas about "tendrils" of health and the analogy of "green shoots" leaning toward sunlight concern arrested aspects of development that are not dead but rather are stymied and are "reaching out"—and, in some fashion seeking to make contact with mirroring, idealizing, and twinship experiences. Can we see this outreach? And, how to respond?

In Chapter Seven, in Dr. Steinman's treatment of Jonathan and the twinship selfobject transference that took hold, we further discuss the contribution that Stern (1985, 2010), along with other infant researchers and psychologists have made to the understanding of "amodal perception," and "cross modal perception." In the above vignette of Dr. Potter and Iris, one now enters the realm of "cross modal attunement."

With all of Kohut's "normalizing" of narcissism, his putting it into a developmental context gives us a better grasp of how it works in the recovery from psychosis. The idea of being "trapped in the mirror" (Golomb, 1992) provides another useful analogy for how Judith, Rachel, Lois, Steven, and the other cases considered in this book can result in myriad forms of psychosis. As those tendrils of health reach out, will they find mirroring, idealizing or alikeness experiences that begin a revitalization process? How does that happen?

In the *Interpersonal World of the Infant* (1985), Stern comes to a slightly different, but quite overlapping understanding than Kohut vis a vis the development of self. He separates this developmental process into four stages: an emergent self, core self, subjective self, and verbal self. Vitality affects sit in a central way to the "emerging self." Stern comments:

> there are many different sensorimotor schemas that need to be adapted, and the consolidation process for each of them involves a subjective experience of somewhat different vitality affects associated with different body parts and sensations in different contexts … It is these subjective experiences of various organizations in formation that I am calling the sense of an emergent self. (Stern, 1985, p. 60)

It is noteworthy that in the following stage, a "core self," self psychology finds important reference to what ails many patients and particularly those with psychosis: loss of self-agency; loss of self coherence; loss of self affectivity and loss of self history or continuity. Furthermore, it is amazing how these are met, one by one, with what Stolorow and Lachmann (1980) see as the function of selfobjects!

Stern notes "it is only in major psychosis that we see a significant absence of any of these four self-experiences" (Stern, 1985, p. 71). He continues: "The sharing of affective states is the most pervasive and clinically germane feature of inter-subjective relatedness … inter-affectivity is mainly what is meant when clinicians speak of parental 'mirroring' and empathic responsiveness" (ibid., p. 138).

Steps involved in "inter-affectivity"

1. Grasp the expressed feeling state from the patient's overt behavior. (Iris's frustration/annoyance with Dr. Potter's inattentiveness).
2. Meet and stay with the same contour of the vitality affect (a pulled punch) but respond, in a de-aggressivitized way, with a slightly different combination/mode. For example, meet a gesture (Iris's swing at Potter) with a verbal response ("Wanna fight" in a teasing friendly tone). The staccato "wanna fight" is similar to Iris's "pulled jab" in terms of intensity, duration and rhythm.
3. Contextualize the exchange with reference to what is most likely to have stirred the patient's dysphoric/euphoric mood. (Upset with not being allowed to see mom—arranging for a "referee." Referee and mitts continue the boxing metaphor in a non-aggressive fashion).

Jack paging the doctor

Let's look at one more example of cross modal attunement (Garfield, 2009):

> A 30 year old Catholic painter, we'll call him Jack, felt that a friend of his from art school had turned the New York City Police against him. In fact, even when he moved to Chicago, the FBI had arranged for him to be constantly monitored and threatened with violence. Now, the Chicago Police were involved. He continued with his artwork but these powerful forces continually undermined his attempts at employment, as an art teacher. Violence was all around him. He had been in treatment before with the therapist who had taken a counter projective stance (Havens, 1986). Here, the attackers are attacked verbally by the therapist as an attempt at "empathy with rage" (Garfield & Havens, 1991). After obtaining some relief, the patient left the area to stay with friends in another state. The therapist wondered if the move was precipitated by

the humiliation that the patient experienced in having to ask his family for money for the treatment.

One year later, the patient returned and the forces of harassment and destruction were as much with him as ever. Would he ever find safe harbor? The clinician lowered the fee. Jack began to page the therapist once a day. At first, the therapist called back right away and said, "Hello, this is Dr. Garfield." In a monotone voice, Jack slowly and calmly replied, that the threats were very bad—then there would be a discussion of some kind and they would hang up. After a month or so, the therapist realized that that he had been thrown off track. Jack sounded completely calm. The clinician was annoyed that he was being paged for something about which the patient seemed affectivity nonplussed. What kind of countertransference was this? Was this an over-exacting demand? Was this the clinician's denial of his own neediness? Was this a projective identification of the patient's own annoyance at the doctor and, if so, for what?

The doctor stopped returning the pages in a timely fashion. It was a case of the little boy who "whispered" wolf. There was no cry. Yet, something was off. So, when Jack paged the doctor, the doctor started calling back immediately and, now, out of breath would loudly query "JACK! Are you OK?" Invariably, Jack would respond: "yes, I'm OK" or "I guess so." Then and only then, the therapist slowed down his tempo and proceeded in a calm way. Yet, it seemed that this new response pattern calmed Jack down a great deal. Once, the cross-modal attunement of dialing the pager was met by the vocal intensity, timing and duration of the return call, the situation began to improve a great deal. Why? This was not a one-time event. The psychiatrist came to realize that Jack was almost always in an inner state of constant panic. Here we have an oscillation between the experience of a tentative cohesion and a sense that horror and destruction are at the front door. Here is Kohut's (1971) annihilation anxiety. The intervention, which eased the situation, was one where, via the use of cross-modal vitality affects, attunement to the patient's paging panic (and relief) was achieved. (Garfield, 2009, p. 119)

With cross modal attunement as our "entre" for making contact with elements of the nascent self in psychosis, let's begin our journey into the evolution of how selfobject experiences facilitate the healing process.

PART I

MIRRORING

CHAPTER ONE

The opening phase—the case of Judith

Judith was a lithe, petite, blue eyed blonde woman in her early twenties when Dr. Steinman first met her in a psychiatry emergency room; blood oozed from four deep self inflicted cuts on her left forearm. She was sitting demurely in an uncomfortable wooden chair, her face bland and remote. Dr. Steinman began ….

"What happened?" Dr. Steinman asked her.
"Nothing."
He persisted: "Surely something happened."
"I don't know" She remained impassive.
"Did something bother you?"
"Uh huh," she responded in a meek, barely perceptible voice.
"What was it?"
"I didn't feel good."
"Where?"
"Here," and she pointed to her abdomen.
Dr. Steinman wanted to continue this developing line of exploration. Why, he wondered, would she cut herself? There must be a lot bothering this very young looking woman; even though her

voice was calm and timorous, cutting herself was an emotion filled act—or one intended to stop emotions.

But the blood was seeping onto the floor of the shabby emergency room Dr. Steinman had begun to work at three weeks earlier at the end of his psychiatry residency. He had trained at a hospital that had a rather large staff for the psychiatry emergency room. But now, trying to support his young family, he was working with only a nurse's aide on duty with him. Before the blood became a problem, Dr. Steinman walked Judith across the street to a fully operational hospital emergency room where her wounds were sutured and butterflies applied.

After Judith's cuts were cared for, he pursued the conversation.

"Has there been any recent change in your life?"

"No; I don't think so."

"Do you live alone?"

"With roommates."

"Everything okay there?"

"Yeah."

"Anyone leave? Or go away on vacation?"

"My psychiatrist has been away for two weeks."

"Have you seen him for long?"

"I've seen her for five years."

"How often do you see her?"

"Oh, every day; and in group too."

"Any thoughts or feelings about your psychiatrist being away?"

"No" as she averted her eyes.

Even then, Dr. Steinman had seen a number of people in the crisis clinic or hospital who were upset about the absence of a treating therapist. In general, he knew that Judith must be reacting to her psychiatrist's vacation; this would be even more likely with such a strong—five days a week—therapeutic involvement.

Her looking away seemed pertinent; he'd often noticed that people who were very upset frequently looked away when they had complicated thoughts and feelings they were unwilling or unable to divulge.

"You mentioned that you had some feelings when you cut yourself, feelings in your abdomen. What were they like?"

"I don't know; just feelings."

"Happy, sad, nervous, tense, lonely, angry? Maybe something else? What do you think?"

"I guess sad and lonely."

"Any idea what that was about? Were you thinking of anything or anyone in particular at the time?"

"Well, I miss my psychiatrist" Judith said, looking at the floor and sighing; "And I wish she'd hurry back; she'll be here in three more days."

"Do you think your cutting yourself had anything to do with missing her and maybe some other feelings about your psychiatrist?"

"Maybe; I haven't really thought about it."

How can someone do something so self-destructive without any understanding of her actions I wondered to myself.

This is the essence of an exploratory psychodynamic psychotherapy, to help a person understand his or her life history and to bring into consciousness previously unconscious material, such as fantasies, wishes and feelings; an intensive psychotherapy that connects the dots between what goes on inside and behavior can lead to transformation, healing, perhaps even a cure.

Affect: the circulatory system of the self

Affects circulate through the mind like blood circulates through the body. With Judith, Dr. Steinman is absorbed by both and he engages both. He immediately notices how, in the midst of her body losing this vital substance that Judith's self appears to have lost the vital substance of its affectivity—she expresses no distress, no anger, no embarrassment, but rather her face is bland and her facial expression, remote.

From the vantage point of self psychology, if an analytic/therapeutic relationship is to be established, the doctor must engage the patient at an affective level. Whereas in neurosis, pain is often contained, in psychosis it can spurt all over—hallucinations, word salad, delusional proclamations or, in Judith's case, grossly disorganized behavior. One must actively get a firm grasp on the where and what of emotion in acute states like this and Judith's affect was in her body's bleeding. Thus, Dr. Steinman tends to her mind by first tending to her body because that is where the vital component of her body/mind/spirit-her self-resides.

First, her cuts. All four of them. But there is more. As all doctors inquire as to where the pain is, so does Dr. S. and he immediately finds out that it is in her abdomen. The reason that self psychologists define the self in terms of body, spirit, and mind is due to the ongoing co-mingling of their ingredients. Central to the clinical endeavor of psychoanalytic self psychology in psychosis, is subjectivity, and central to the concept of subjectivity is the notion of "feelings." Feelings, of course, must be "felt" and if they are felt, they must be felt somewhere. That somewhere is the body. Here we have the most "experience near" location of subjectivity, the body. Exactly what was Judith feeling in her abdomen?

A language for emotion: from the outside to the inside

It is well known in psychiatry and psychology, that the inability to express emotions in words-alexithymia—is closely associated with psychosomatic disorders (Nemiah & Sifneos, 1970). Judith doesn't feel good in her abdomen—Dr. Steinman wants her to get more specific. Notice how in the investigation of the precipitating event, Dr. Steinman attempts to first collect the who, what, where, when, and how of what has recently afflicted the patient. He asks about people who might be important to her like roommates, but all is well on that front. However, she mentions that her psychiatrist is away. In wanting her to get more specific with her feeling experience, he gives her a menu of feeling words and she picks lonely and sad. It could be argued that this collection of external data violates one of the primary modes of knowing about the patient vis a vis the tenets of self psychology, that is, empathy and vicarious introspection. Yet, these kinds of "objective" questions are actually perquisite to vicarious introspection and empathic attunement. Without knowing the specific circumstances of where the patient has lost their footing, it impossible to put oneself in their "shoes." Thus, an exploration of the precipitating event is the first step of an empathic process. Once the clinician obtains this vicarious balance, he is much more able to reflect on how it feels to be in those shoes. The clinician, through this process of attunement, engages his own affects as imagined and will use these as the basis for establishing rapport or a feeling connection to the patient.

Modern neuropsychology might point to the ubiquity of "mirror neurons" (Gallese, 2001) as being vital to our ability to develop empathy. Here, when an other's behavior is observed, "mirror neurons" fire adjacent to those very same motor neurons responsible for the observed movement inside our own brains. Perhaps, mentally "going through the motion" without enacting it allows us to better understand the emotion of the patient. At the very least, we develop an orientation to the position of the patient in their own world as we imagine it. Interestingly, there may be a separate set of "mirror neurons" specifically for emotion (Gallese, 2001).

This "front of mind" awareness of the body in psychosis is a slightly different focus for self psychologists who typically work with neurotic or borderline patients. Because the circulatory system of the self is one of affects and because the extreme fragmentation, discontinuity and loss of a positive state of well being (Stolorow & Lachmann, 1980) is pathognomonic of psychotic states, it becomes incumbent upon the analyst to quickly locate and secure these feelings in the body. As Freud (1923) emphasized, the first ego is a body ego. For self psychologists, these affect body locations are the vital signs of the self and, therefore, are one of our first orders of business.

Self reflection and mobilization into an analytic process

Dr. Steinman was a psychiatrist who came to psychoanalysis already prepared for the "widening scope of analysis" (Stone, 1954) convinced that an intensive psychoanalytic psychotherapy would help even the most disturbed.

Yet, here was Judith—with five years of daily supportive/educational therapy—cutting herself and blandly reporting that she had no idea why she did it. Being a little annoyed that someone could be so oblivious to her motivation—Dr. Steinman reflected that he wasn't sure if he was irritated at her or her therapist. He wanted to see if Judith could understand that cutting herself was associated with feelings that were uncomfortable to her.

> "Have you ever cut yourself before?"
> The answer was not so surprising.
> "When I was in the hospital and they gave me shock treatment, I cut HURT on my stomach."

> "What made you do that?"
>
> "I don't know," she said softly.
>
> "Did you discuss it with your psychiatrist or the hospital staff?"
>
> "No, we never talked about it."

For most analysts, the central purpose of psychiatric treatment is to help people understand themselves; yet, according to Judith, the patient's psychiatrist and the hospital staff hadn't inquired into the meaning of her cutting. Most psychiatrists believe that there isn't much you can do with very disturbed people except give them medications and place them in groups or day hospitals. Most analysts believe there is meaning in a person's actions, thoughts, hallucinations, and delusions and try to decipher these meanings, using medication judiciously. It has been suggested (Ellenberger, 1970), that psychoanalysis contains both an investigative and a therapeutic impulse. There are those clinicians who focus on the "why" and those who don't and who primarily care, simply, that things get better. Psychoanalysis, as Ellenberger pointed out grew out of the belief that the investigative process was curative. Here, "making the unconscious conscious" was the therapeutic mechanism of change. Yet, psychoanalytic self psychology comes at cure slightly differently. Although, self understanding and interpretation are necessary ingredients, they are not sufficient. Something else is required. In "How does analysis cure" (1984), Kohut points out that it is a "strengthening of the self" that is essential to healing. As Tolpin (2002) points out, this occurs through a re-engaging of the thwarted developmental emotional needs of the patient. Later, we will discuss more about the therapeutic mechanism by which psychotic patients emerge from the grip of their hallucinations and delusions, but first, the restoration of patient's full "self circulatory system" requires that affects must be engaged.

> As their first encounter progressed, Dr. Steinman figured that he would try a slightly different tack from the one to which Judith was accustomed.
>
> "You cut yourself four times; does that have any meaning for you? Why four and not some other number? What does four mean to you?"
>
> "I don't know," Judith said vaguely, then stopped short and looked perplexed; she was not accustomed to exploring the meaning of her behavior. She hadn't questioned, she merely

acted. Then, slowly, she said, I guess it reminds me of being four years old.

"What was going on in your life at the age of four?"

Again, she had no idea. But she was physically OK for the time being and Dr. Steinman didn't expect to see her again since she had such a long standing and intense relationship with her therapist; He wished her well, told her that the emergency room was open twenty-four hours a day, and that she should return if she ran into trouble before her psychiatrist came back.

Evidently, several months later, Judith began to discuss, with her therapist and parents, the idea of beginning treatment with Dr. Steinman.

Several months after that, when the treating psychiatrist concurred, Judith and her parents contacted Dr. S. and she began an analytic psychotherapy aimed at clarifying and understanding her thoughts and behavior within the context of her life's experiences, emotions and psychological ways of dealing with pain. It became an effort that revealed much more clearly what her thinking was and how it arose.

The previous therapist had viewed Judith as essentially psychotic and in need of supportive care, for she had several diagnoses of acute, now chronic schizophrenia, on both psychiatric assessment and psychological testing.

Such a "supportive" treatment approach is anything but supportive of the individual. "Supportive" treatment can lead to warehousing—putting patients in custodial care where their symptoms may be less but the beliefs persist; it is an attempt to cover over the symptoms and disordered thinking. Sometimes it works and the psychosis goes into apparent remission, leaving the patient in a fragile condition dependent on medication and often regressing when unresolved issues erupt and overwhelm them; sometimes this covering over approach doesn't work at all.

Almost all psychoanalytic treatments believe in the idea that normal development can run into problems and become "fixated," "arrested" or "derailed." Classical psychoanalysis, ego psychology, and the object relations schools of psychoanalysis go at this process all pretty much from the same point of view expressed by Freud in "Recommendations to physicians on beginning the treatment" (Freud, 1915). Approach the patient from the surgical point of view … from the "outside" going "in." Of course you must first put the patient to sleep. In psychoanalysis, the analogy is "fostering a regression to the point of fixation." Here, the analyst analyzes defenses, keeps the patient lying down and slowly does the dissection until the wound, in its entirety, is encountered. After it is fully explored, cleaned out and set right through the process of reliving the pain of the transference and establishing a better adaptation (the traditional transference interpretation and "working through" process) then it naturally heals and the analyst/surgeon heads out again through the termination process.

Yet, consistent with an "inside/out" orientation that is the hallmark of self psychology, the self psychologist of psychosis approaches the whole process in a very different fashion. The basic idea is different and this difference has enormous implications for how one thinks about the entire treatment process.

Psychopathology and self psychology

Self psychology views pathology as breakdown products of early developmental arrest. At each stage of development there is a whole self, meeting developmental challenges insofar as its attempts to obtain needed responsiveness from essential environmental resources are successful. When these needed resources are either not present or are aversive, then development cannot proceed. Using the analogy of the self being an emerging "garden," if there is no water or sunlight then the "plant withers on the vine." Depending on the degree of differentiation and hierarchic integration at which this "trauma" occurs, the resulting appearance will vary.

Unique to the viewpoint of self psychology is the notion that though the individual child may be blocked or hurt, there remain, inside, "tendrils" of self that continue to seek out conditions that will permit the resumption of growth. In her landmark work of 2002, Marian Tolpin described "the psychoanalysis of normal development" wherein she explicated these "forward edge transferences" through which analysis cures.

A new view of transference

Tolpin expands the transference continuum to include "the trailing edge," the "intermediate" area and "the forward edge" of the total transference. The "trailing edge" is that which is familiar to all analysts and therapists. Here, painful repetitions of early trauma are reawakened by excessive frustration. The "intermediate area" consists of "symptomatic" expressions of transference wherein wishes/fears, defenses, painful affects and superego elements combine in well understood ways in enactments and symptoms. The "forward edge" is comprised of the buried ongoing attempts to derive needed responsiveness from encounters that are either affirming, securing or alikeness experiences. Here is where Tolpin locates Kohut's selfobject transferences on the spectrum of the total transference.

How does analysis cure psychosis?

How is the treatment of psychosis approached differently by self psychology rather than other psychoanalytic approaches? The idea is that if self-esteem is facilitated by an effective engagement with the "forward edge" then restoration of the self will take place through a progressive strengthening process. Maladaptive defensive maneuvers can be interpreted without reawakening negative affect laden "trailing edge" experiences. Disappointment and inevitable empathic failures of the analyst are also addressed differently. Here, the analyst takes responsibility for the lapses while at the same time exploring the negative fragmentation and symptomatic eruptions that are the result. This acknowledgement works to restore a cohesive self and the strengthening process takes place as Wolf (1988) describes through cycles of "disruption and repair."

With Judith, the "supportive" approach had failed terribly, no matter how much medication she took or how much reality oriented activity she was involved in. Nowhere in this previous approach with Judith was there the possibility for self understanding and a strengthening of her self, other than to say that "these are delusions or hallucinations" and she should keep them to herself. As far as Dr. Steinman could tell, an in depth oriented approach had not been tried. She had been considered hopeless.

We believe that there is no such thing as a hopeless psychiatric patient. It seems that every patient we've seen has the possibility of improvement, perhaps healing—maybe even cure, through a psychotherapy aimed at understanding the current situation in light of past experiences, hopes, fears, and wishes. There is nothing more necessary for the severely disturbed psychiatric patient than HOPE, the possibility of unwinding the disorder, of putting the pain and chaos behind and of becoming less isolated and feeling more human.

Judith: developmental history

Judith was the middle child of a prosperous family. The father was stern and preoccupied with business, yet caring. He tried to get the kids to work with him, but to little avail. He tended to be guilt inducing and would mutter, "remember Uncle Bill"—his brother who had died young—whenever the kids would fight.

The mother was supportive, flighty, and overly self-indulgent. When Judith was an infant, the mother had reamed out the nipple of the baby bottle, so that the child would more quickly get her milk (and the mother would have to deal with less noise and difficulty). Until the age of three, the mother put her to bed early every night with bottles of juice; since she wasn't tired she remembers fantasizing for what seemed like long periods until she fell asleep. At the age of four, her mother let her stay home from kindergarten for six months, when she inexplicably appeared terrified about leaving her mother and began vomiting at school.

A two-year older sister and a three-and-a-half-year younger brother rounded out the family picture. Judith remembers battles with her sister who got more attention and hating her brother who got so much more attention than either of the two girls. Her father's parents died before her birth, her maternal grandfather had committed suicide just prior to her turning six; her maternal grandmother died while she was in college.

Dr. Steinman's office, in those days, was sparsely furnished, reflecting his straightened circumstances after ten years of graduate education. Patients sat in an old Morris chair he had lovingly spent three days refinishing before going into practice. He sat in an intricately carved oak rocking chair. Both chairs had home-made cushions. This was no "white coat" environment.

To the side was an old steamer trunk from his wife's family. Desks seemed to confer unnecessary solemnity and status to the doctor in what was basically an inquiry between two people. On the trunk was an ancient silver teapot and several cups, one for each person. Flowers from his garden sat on the trunk and—being California—brightened the room in all seasons.

In an alcove sat a perfect Freudian couch ... Various knick-knacks graced the mantelpiece. Interesting rocks, a child's sculpture, a vase for flowers; anything could be there, depending on the situation.

In this environment, some patients launch in with all sorts of material about their life; some find the going more difficult. With these people, questions about what makes it difficult to talk are often helpful.

> At first Judith spoke haltingly, if at all, as she sat demurely in the Morris chair. She invariably wore jeans and large collared polo shirts of different pastels. Ira would alternately sit quietly, at times rocking, or engage her about herself and her life; the goal was always to try to find out how she got to be who she was. What might have appeared to the casual observer to be a conversation was actually an attempt to clarify and understand her disturbance, as the preliminary to treatment and change.
>
> "How's it going today?"
> "Ok."
> "Anything happening?"
> "Not much. My roommate went back in the hospital."
> "What happened?"
> "She got suicidal. Her psychiatrist decided she should be in the hospital."
> "Did that bother you?"
> "Yeah. I worry about her." Judith looked pensive.
> "What are you worried about?"
> "If she really would try to kill herself again."
> "Has she tried?"
> "Oh yes. A bunch of times."
> "Why does she try?"
> "I don't know."
> "Does she know?"
> "I don't think so."
> "Any ideas as to why she gets suicidal?"
> "No." Judith looks away, down at the floor. She appears to be getting more upset as we sit, looking frightened, at times trembling. She glances furtively over her right shoulder.
> "What are you looking at?" he asked her.
> "Nothing."
> "Looks like you're looking at something."

> In the most confidential of tones, she hesitatingly begins. "She's there."
>
> "Who?"
>
> "The Good Angel."
>
> "Who's she?"
>
> "You don't see her?"
>
> "No I don't see her; but I can see that you're looking at something. Who is the Good Angel? What's she like?"

This is such an important point in the therapy of very disturbed people. Judith is willing to tell one of her closely guarded secrets, indicating her faith in the process. Such an offering of a secret may be the beginning of driving a wedge between her and her delusional beliefs. The hope is always that rationality and comprehension will gradually take the place of blind belief. In practice, the beginning of such a change is the understanding of "The Good Angel."

Psychoanalytic inquiry: empathy

Psychoanlaysis was born out of neurology and not unexpectedly relied on the idea that the brain was an association making machine. That each individual's private world was based on the unique pattern of experience that links one thought, one memory, one smell (perception) or one feeling to another. By extension, in psychosis, one would want to know the way delusions and hallucinations link together with the above mental experiences as well. Thus, the main mode of inquiry and understanding was via understanding how one experience is associated with another. Indeed, as Ellenberger pointed out (1970), psychoanalysis derived out of Hebart's "associational psychology."

Although empathy—putting oneself into the patient's "shoes," was always an important tool in the analyst's toolbox, it had always remained in the background until Kohut's groundbreaking work of 1959 "Introspection, empathy and psychoanalysis: An examination of the relationship between mode of observation and theory." Here and in his subsequent contribution "Beyond the bounds of the basic rule" (1960), Kohut begins the shift in theory that would lead to the development of self psychology. The key shift at this point was the fact that the most important way of understanding patients was not by figuring out what their associations revealed about their mind but rather understanding how they were feeling. Once the analyst could imagine how the patient must be feeling, there was another technical element that needed to be followed. Kohut advised that once the analyst collected the history of the patient's current and past situation, he needed to "go inside himself" to find something—no matter how small or different—that had a similar feel to it, which the analyst had experienced. Only then, could the analyst "know" how it felt to be this patient and only then could the patient "be known." Later, Kohut would suggest that this empathy, this vicarious introspection, this knowing the patient was not only central to understanding the patient but, in addition, this "in depth" understanding of the patient was also central to the curative process.

The history of the delusion and hallucination

It is crucial now to try to take a history of the delusional being and how it developed. Therein lies the opportunity for comprehension and collaboration. To merely say that a delusional belief is psychotic and add more medicines is antithetical to the possibility of transformation.

> "She's a woman in white flowing robes."
> "How old?"
> "Oh, forty or forty-five."
> "What's she like?"
> "She's very nice."
> "Does she say anything or just sit there?"
> "She tells me to do all kinds of good things; she's the Good Angel."
> "Like what?"
> "To cut myself, or hurt myself."

For years the angel, which Judith could see and hear, had dictated to her what she should do. Judith would converse with this presence much of the time, even when talking with other people. This accounted for the engrossed daydreaming look and flattened emotions that had been noted in psychiatric records over the years. Had no one seriously attempted to ask about where her attention went during this obvious withdrawal from day to day reality?

The "Good Angel" told Judith to do things that were, to her mind, "good" for herself, such as cut her wrists. The "good angel" had persisted since adolesence when it had told her to cut herself and she had carved "HURT" on her abdomen.

Gradually, with a bit of prodding and questioning, Judith elaborated her history with the "Good Angel." The "Good Angel" was her master. When she cut herself, took overdoses or threatened to jump from the Golden Gate Bridge, she was following the precepts of "the Good Angel."

These self-destructive acts were "good" things to do to herself, for she was "such a terrible person," and had been so for nearly as long as she could remember, certainly back to kindergarten. She had known she was "such a terrible person" since kindergarten, even before the "Good Angel" had developed.

> "When did you start to believe you were such a terrible person?"
> "five or six."
> "What made you believe that?"
> "I don't know. I just am."

Psychotherapy works in fits and starts. A person often isn't able to just answer direct questions; historical events, feelings and interactions may be hidden from consciousness. As we talk and resistances to awareness are dealt with, more information gradually becomes available. What is unknown today, hidden under layers of repression or segmented off into realms of disavowal, may become available as the work continues and as fears of retraumatization recede. Dr. Steinman asked Judith about her badness, wondered why she felt so terrible and thought so ill of herself. For her it was a given that she was bad, or evil, for the "Good Angel" told her so. She had no sense as to why this might be the case.

Psychiatrists, therapists and analysts have the reputation of being non-judgmental; but are quite judgmental when it comes to belief in delusional beings that, unchecked, may lead to harm and death.

Dr. Steinman began to cast doubt on the "Good Angel" which wanted her to hurt and be punished. He questioned how "good" could have such negative consequences. He inquired as to how a "good" angel could urge her to do such self-destructive things. He began to ask a lot of questions and wondered if there were in fact angels. Could her belief in angels be a relic of her early religious upbringing? Did such a belief in a woman in her mid twenties say various things about her, about a regression to a younger self and an attempt on her part to stay away from her own history and feelings and experiences? How did the angel begin?

This is a delicate time in any psychotherapy. Delusions, fantasies and all sorts of pieces of mental content often serve a self-protective, self soothing or self enhancing purpose and "taking them away" may have serious unintended consequences. In addition, it is important to maintain a working alliance with a patient. How do you do this, when you are essentially telling someone that they are mistaken?

The best way is to take a history from the delusional figure. How did the "Good Angel" develop, and in what circumstances? Judith was extremely vague about the origin of her protecting demiurge, able to say only that she began in high school. Hopefully, the questioning itself would begin to loosen her firm conviction of the "Good Angel's" existence and benefit to her, as rationality shed some light on—and slowly supplanted—blind belief. As we will hear later on, self psychology sees delusions slightly differently than other psychoanalytic approaches. Here Kohut's ideas about a "vertical split" in consciousness come to the foreground. The delusion helps fill a narcissistic deficit.

After several months of trying to surround and undermine the belief in the "Good Angel" with questions about the "Good Angel's" reality, morality, existence, and meaning, Dr. Steinman witnessed another momentous change with Judith.

> In session, Judith sat quietly for several minutes, then began shaking. She was clearly frightened, apprehensively looking over her left shoulder. She tried to whisper, but couldn't; she tried to point to her left shoulder but her trembling index finger failed her.
> "You look upset; what's bothering you?"
> "I'm not sure," she quavered.
> "You're looking over your left shoulder. Is anything there?"
> "You don't see him?" She barely whispered.
> "No. Who do you see?"
> "Him, the Bad Devil."
> "What's he like?"
> "A grown man, with dark curly hair."
> "What's he wearing?"
> "A red devil suit."
> "Where does he live?"
> "Only over my left shoulder."
> "What does the left shoulder mean?"
> "Sinister."

"What does he want?"
"He wants bad things for me. He wants me to do bad things."
"Like what?"
"I don't know."
"Ask him."

Dr. Steinman seeks to bring this piece of psychic structure into the analytic dialogue with Judith.

After a minute in which she tentatively asks him out loud what he wants for her, Judith looks puzzled. "He says he wants me to enjoy myself, have friends, go to school or work and have a boyfriend."

"So tell me, how is this bad?"

She looks rather sheepish. "I'm not sure."

"You're really confused between good and bad. A 'Good Angel' wants you to hurt yourself and a 'Bad Devil' wants good things for you. The bad in the guise of the good is on your right shoulder. The good in the guise of the bad is on your left or sinister shoulder. You've got some rethinking to do."

Judith talked about who the "bad devil" might represent. Slowly she was able to understand that it represented Dr. Steinman, or a more positive aspect of herself. This became confusing, for she was under the sway and domination of the "good angel" which wanted her to be punished. If punishment was good and enjoyment bad, she must be very mixed up. This confusion was difficult for her. If good was bad, and bad good, her psychological life had been turned inside out. Not just inside out, but, since it was so upsetting, it had been placed outside of herself in the personages of angels and devils.

These issues were explored four times per week in psychotherapy; the frequency of our visits was an attempt to help her get a handle on the emerging material. Sometimes, Judith was extremely suicidal; sometimes she would cut at her arms or legs with razors or a knife as she tried to wrap her mind around the concept of the "Good Angel" being malign when she ordered Judith to cut herself.

Pressing for recognition: multiple personality

Dr. Steinman was a little surprised to see Judith sitting demurely on a burgundy sofa in the waiting room an hour before her appointment, when he asked another patient to come in. Judith was reading a magazine and had several other magazines scattered over the sofa. After the patient went into his office, he asked Judith if she was okay; she said she was fine.

"Why so early?"

"Oh, I was in the neighborhood and figured it'd be easier to wait here."

"You're sure you're okay?" Dr. Steinman was concerned because this was so out of character for her. She was punctual—much more so then he. But an hour early seemed strange to him.

"I'm fine" she insisted.

"Knock on the door if you're upset." Dr. Steinman couldn't get out of his mind the sense that something was not quite right.

"Okay" she said sweetly.

She didn't knock on the door. When he went to the waiting room to get her an hour later, she was still sitting demurely on the burgundy sofa.

"What the hell is this!"

"What?" she said softly.

"The blood all over the magazines!"

"I don't know." She seemed out of touch, showing little emotion.

"Let me see your arms" he ordered, his anger rising.

Her arms were covered with magazines. Sure enough, under the magazines, blood oozed from cuts she had made in her left arm while she cut with a razor in her right hand. Dr. Steinman quickly went to the bathroom to get some paper towels to staunch the blood.

"Jesus Christ!"

Blood was everywhere on the floor, the sink, the tiles. She had obviously cut herself in the bathroom, then returned to the sofa.

"Why did you do this?" he asked as he held some towels to her bleeding arm.

"She told me to do it" Judith said matter of factly.

"Who?"

"The Good Angel" she said coyly.

He could tell by the unclotted nature of the blood that she had just cut herself between the time his previous patient left and he had come to get her.

> He exploded. "What is the matter with you? You couldn't knock on the door? I don't care how upset you were or what 'The Good Angel' told you, you check with me first. There is no circumstance in which you are allowed to cut yourself. You're coming with me to the hospital."
>
> "I'm okay."
>
> "It is not okay to cut yourself. It is not okay to believe that an imaginary person is telling you to cut yourself just because you are having trouble handling feelings. Why did you really cut yourself?"
>
> "I don't know."
>
> "Maybe you'll figure it out in the hospital. Let's go."

Most would agree that Dr. Steinman was in the middle of a countertransference reaction. He was anything but his usual calm self. He was heated and angry with Judith. The primary reason he believed, was that he had asked her to knock on the door and she wouldn't even do that to look after herself. In a very strong, emotional way he was chastising her for her not being protective of herself.

She had cut herself on a number of other occasions at her home. At Dr. Steinman's urging, she had brought in the scissors, knives, pins, and razors with which she had cut herself. They had been able to talk about her underlying feelings as they explored the reasons for her self mutilations, her difficulty handling feelings and dealing with the psychological changes required of her in beginning to look at her self-destructiveness and her belief in the "Good Angel" who was bad for her.

During each of these previous explorations, he had maintained a psychiatric detachment. He was furious that she had followed the directions of a self destructive hallucination and not listened to his protective admonitions to let him know if she was upset.

> As they walked the several blocks to the hospital, she reached down for a piece of glass. He grabbed her hand.
>
> "You will not do that any longer. This cutting is not okay. I don't care what the 'Good Angel' is saying to you or how badly you're feeling; there is no reason to cut yourself. You will talk it through without acting on it! You will stop harming yourself or you'll call me right away to help you work it through. This is just how it's going to be!"

She nodded, quietly.

They went to the emergency room to have her cuts dealt with and arranged for a short psychiatric hospital admission. Dr. Seinman later got a call from the medical doctor who was seeing her.

"I've never seen a happier patient."

"What do you mean?" Dr. Steinman asked uncomprehendingly.

"She was almost bragging about how you swore at her and told her she could never cut herself again. She told all the nurses and me how worked up you got. She's been positively beaming about it."

Dr. Steinman felt that his outburst showed her that he really cared about her. From the point of view of "the inside out," Judith felt noticed, affirmed, and important. These are the tendrils of a "mirroring selfobject experience." Judith never cut herself again. Dr. Steinman's "countertransference" reaction was spontaneous and unplanned. Obviously, it meant a lot to Judith. But an important question emerges. What effect did his behavior have on the inside of the patient? What does it mean to feel that someone "really cares" and what does that say about Judith's psychological self?

The mirror transference

Through his work with narcissistic personality disorders, Kohut (1971) began to understand some of the ways in which these patients do not form "usual" transferences but rather "narcissistic transferences." Their bond to the analyst took on one of two kinds of qualities. Either the patient seemed to require that the analyst provide an ongoing stream of admiration, recognition, and affirmation or the patient seemed to require that the analyst be all knowing, reassuring, and powerful. Disturbances in these unconscious expectations would lead to significant disruption in the patient's psychic economy until the ship was righted.

Kohut futher recognized that these patients were missing an internal ability to provide themselves with these kinds of experiences and unconsciously "bonded" with the analyst so as to absorb these needed kind of responses. Rather than being unconsciously re-experienced as a specific person from the past, as in the traditional transferences, these unconscious experiences focused on self-esteem and self regulation. He first labeled these as "self-object transferences" (later dropping the hyphen). The need for the analyst to affirm, recognize and admire, were called "mirroring selfobject transferences"; those that required the analyst to be strong, all knowing and perfect were labeled as "idealizing" selfobject transferences. Later, as his exploration continued, Kohut identified a third selfobject experience which seemed to be missing in some of these patients. This involved needing the analyst to be "like" the patient. Here was the "twinship" selfobject experience.

As this nascent self psychology evolved, Kohut postulated that normal, primary, narcissism worked differently than Freud (1912) had originally hypothesized. Rather than narcissism advancing through stages of autoeroticism to homosexuality to heterosexuality ("I love me" to "I love people like me" to "I love people who are opposite or who complement me"), Kohut first saw narcissism as evolving along its own developmental line to more mature forms of narcissism in a fashion parallel to Freud's psychosexual developmental schema. In the forms and transformations of narcissism (1966), Kohut had already conjectured that the more advanced forms of narcissism yielded creativity, empathy, transience, humor, and wisdom.

Given this evolving understanding of narcissism, Kohut came to understand that there was a normal "bipolar" self that built strength and solidity through two potential sources. One was through a line of experiences of recognition (the "grandiose" self) and the other through a line of being under the "wing" of a perfect other (the idealized parent imago). Grandiosity led to normal healthy ambitions when it was integrated into the developing psyche and idealizing led to ideals, as incremental integration took place at that pole as well. Knowing that developmental experiences are never completely smooth in either providing seamless affirmation or perfect responsivity and role modeling, Kohut created the idea of "selfobjects" to fill the usual rends in normal psychic fabric. We are reminded of Browning's famous line (1890) "I love you not for who you are but for what I am when I am with you."

In the opening phase of Dr. Steinman's work with Judith, we see the establishment of a mirroring transference. Judith has tested her analyst and she continues to find him reliable, predicable, and dependable. He is paying attention and although she may continue to test him, she has had manifold experiences of being seen, noticed, and responded to by him.

CHAPTER TWO

Judith—the middle phase*

From Dr. Steinman:

> "During that first year of treatment, I hospitalized Judith for a few short hospitalizations to protect her from her self-destructive carrying out of the 'Good Angel's' edicts. This was done for her own good and also served the function of reality testing; the wishes of the 'good angel' were bad and would be dealt with accordingly. I became the powerful figure who entered her psychic life, not just as the 'bad devil', but as a new protector to protect her from the previous 'protector', the good angel, who actually harmed her.
>
> Little by little Judith's confusion clarified and she reintegrated during this first year of therapy. Good and evil, right and wrong became her own issues, no longer placed outside of herself in the form of imagined and concretized beings. Both 'Good Angel' and 'Bad Devil' disappeared and were no longer in her consciousness."

---

*Part of this chapter is adapted from the article "The vertical split in neurosis and psychosis: Motor acts and the infrastructure of agency," in: *The Psychoanalytic Review, 92*: 2, 249–270 (2005), and is reprinted with permission of the Guildford Publishers.

Taking a step back

When trying to identify whether Judith is developing a mirroring versus an idealizing selfobject transference to Dr. Steinman, one might be tempted to conclude that since he is acting in the role of a "protector," that this means that Judith is mobilizing an idealizing type of needed transference to her therapist. He takes her to the hospital when she is bleeding, he gets angry with her when she is listening to the "good angel" and is hurting herself and at times, he scolds her "for her own good." We get a glimpse, as noted before, as to what is important to Judith in all of this. When at the hospital, she tells the staff with a certain amount of pride that her doctor cares about her, she "comes into being" with being noticed, seen, and valued. We can hear Kohut's remarks as we think about her body dissociations:

> we know that children also enjoy games in which body parts are again isolated—counting toes, for example: 'This little piggy went to market, this little piggy stayed home …' Such games seem to rest on the setting up of slight fragmentation fears at a period when the cohesiveness of the self has not yet become totally entrenched. The tension, however is kept in bounds (like the separation anxiety in the peek-a-boo game) (Kleeman, 1967) and when the last toe is reached, empathic mother and child undo the fragmentation by uniting in laughter and embrace. (Kohut, 1971, pp. 118–119, in Siegel, 1996)

Well, of course Judith's examples are nowhere as benign, yet taking a step back, we can see the analogy. Dr. Steinman keeps her bounded, he is paying attention to her various fragmented experiences and therapist and patient come together as the even greater threat of fragmentation is dissipated.

Yet, it is important to take a step back and look at the movement of the entire treatment and upon closer inspection, we see that Judith is living with a bunch of parts of herself that function in somewhat of a coherent, if dysfunctional and self-destructive kind of fashion. She has constituted these "fantasy selfobjects" which were of a delusional quality. We will explore these phenomena more, later.

Regrouping—the self begins to strengthen

Shortly afterward, Judith returned home for a year and a half, where she worked at a paid job. She had stopped hurting herself, went to therapy once every week or two, and started developing friendships both at home and in San Francisco. Dr. Steinman gradually lowered her antipsychotic medicines, which were now at a level of about a fifth of what she had previously been taking.

> "I wondered if this could be just the tip of the iceberg. Underneath, might lurk a delusional system far more serious, pervasive and debilitating than the superficial layer we had addressed."

Notice in the therapist's voice a certain cautiousness about Judith's real improvement. All through the treatment, Judith's analyst was not about to assume that what he saw on the surface was what was going on in the depths. His intent to "see" what was really happening was a response to what Marian Tolpin (2002) has described as the "leading edge" of selfobject transferences—in Judith's case a "mirroring" one.

After a year and a half at home, Judith felt stronger and returned to San Francisco. Shortly after her return, she strode into the office in an uncharacteristically bold fashion, stood by her chair and started talking to Dr. Steinman in a very assertive way.

> "I'm not going to take any more medicine." Judith said.
>
> "Why not?"
>
> "I don't like them and don't like the way they make me feel; I'm not taking medicines anymore."
>
> "You're taking so much less now; why not continue cutting them down as we have and seeing if you can handle it."
>
> "I'm not taking them anymore. Don't you believe in what you do? You're teaching me to understand things and make sense of everything in me. I'm not going to take any more medicines."
>
> "Ok. We'll try it your way. But if you run into difficulty that we can't handle in the office, you're back on meds and in the hospital, if need be. Agreed?"
>
> "Agreed" she fairly shouted at Dr. Steinman.

Regression in self psychology

After a few sessions on no medications, she came in to the office one afternoon but, instead of sitting in her customary chair, lay on her back on the floor. After several minutes, she began writhing around. Judith scrunched her eyes closed, leaning first in one direction, then another. Her arms were flattened by her sides. Her body slid little by little in a headward direction.

After a suitable time of quietly observing her in hopes that something verbal would come up, Dr. Steinman asked, "What are you doing?"

There was a silence of several minutes, as the gyrations continued. Finally, she said, "I'm giving birth, giving birth to myself."

This continued for several more minutes, with Judith arching and contorting her body as she slowly slithered along on the carpet. Abruptly, she stopped her imagined attempts at negotiating the birth canal; she became still. After a little time, she dramatically and bombastically stated,

"I'm now born in a new way. Nine months from now is my birthday. Nine months from now, I will decide if I will live or die."

The assertiveness and bombast were different from Judith's usual way of being. He asked what was going on, how had she been born. She responded in what seemed to be a parody of a little girl's voice.

"I'm 'Judy'. That's what my big sister calls me. I'm four and a half years old."

Disbelieving, but trying to suspend disbelief, he asked, "How tall are you?"

"Three feet tall" she responded in the same little girl voice.

"What are you wearing?"

"A pink checked dress; my mommy bought it for me."

Dr. Steinman notes: "I sensed a therapeutic dilemma. I didn't want to encourage a delusional orientation, yet wanted to continue the flow of material. I decided to try to ride both horses at once by speaking from the reality of the situation, but trying to elicit more information."

"As far as I can tell, Judith, you're a woman in your mid twenties lying on the floor of my office. Yet you tell me that you're a four-and-a-half-year-old little girl named 'Judy'. What are you trying to tell us?"

She was quiet for a moment. "I don't know."

"Perhaps seeing yourself as 'Judy' is your way of describing feeling states or historical information you have trouble dealing with."

Again, a noncommittal response.

"When did you get the sense that you were two people, one older, one so much younger? Have you read anything, or seen any movies or television shows?"

"No, this is how it has been for nearly as far back as I can remember."

Rather than argue with her, and run the risk of cutting off the flow of material, Dr. Steinman took a history of "Judy" and listened to "Judy's" tale as it emerged over months of sessions. "So, you're four years old. What's going on?"

"I'm having a good time. I play the piano. And she feeds me all that I want."

"Who, your mother?"

"No; she does," Judith replied pointing over her right shoulder.

"Do you mean the 'Good Angel'?"

"No, silly. She's gone" she says with some childlike impatience. "'Mother God' feeds me."

"And who is 'Mother God'?"

"She's this woman."

"Is she your mother?"

"No. They're different."

"How?"

"Well, my mother is home and 'Mother God' is always with me."

"What's 'Mother God' like?"

"She's always with me. She feeds me as much as I want to eat. She keeps me happy."

"How?"

"She feeds me."

"What?"

"Milk."

"And she lives over your right shoulder? Just where the 'Good Angel' lived?"

"Close to where the 'Good Angel' lived; but she's gone now."

"Were they both there together?"

"Sure, but 'Mother God' was first."

"Does she look like anyone you know?"

"No, just a nice woman."

"Hair color?"

"Grey."

"What's your mother's hair color?"

"Grey. But they're not the same. 'Mother God' wears white robes; my mother wears dresses."

"So 'Mother God' isn't a symbol for your mother?"
"No; of course not."
"Why not?"
"Because 'Mother God' has been with me since I was born."
"Oh, when was that?"
"When I was four or four-and-a-half."
"You mean you were never younger than four or four-and-a-half?"
"No. I've always been this age."
"Have you ever gotten older?"
"No, I've always been four or four-and-a-half, three feet tall and wearing a pink, checked dress."
"And you still are?"
"I still am."

Dr. S.: Judith was regressed, but always able to make it to appointments. I was concerned about whether or not she could manage, but she reassured me that she could drive and said she didn't want any hospital or psychiatric day care. I figured I'd see what developed.

Having viewed herself as "Judy," being born in a new way from herself, Judith began to bring up many sucking delusions. With great trepidation, she began to talk, often in a young child's voice, about material that had preoccupied her since early childhood.

At my office, she would lie on the floor, sucking her thumb, and tell me about being filled up with a whitish fluid. At home, she would spend hours, often the greater part of a day, immersed in these productions, certain that they were the most meaningful endeavor in which she might be involved.

"You believe you're sucking on something and being filled with a whitish fluid. What is it?"
"Milk."
"Are you really sucking and being filled with milk?"
"Of course, don't be stupid."
"And what do you look like?"
"I've told you; I'm four years old, three feet tall and I'm wearing a pink checked dress."
"I think you wish you were breastfeeding."
"I remember my brother's birth when I was three-and-a-half and him getting bottles from my mother, and my aunt nursed my

cousin a little while later. My cousin looked so happy." A beatific smile spreads across Judith's face as she describes her cousin's contentment at her aunt's breast.

"How old were you?"

"Four."

Dr. S.: Over a number of sessions, she began to talk about her early family history. Feeling that her mother was unavailable to her with the birth of her brother when Judith was three-and-a-half, Judith began fantasizing sucking a breast or her father's penis in order to get some of the contentment and warmth she felt her infant cousin and brother got from nursing.

She was aware of being angry at her mother for being less attentive to her, with the birth of her brother. She also was angry at her brother, but expressing that was not okay in her family, where her brother superseded her merely because he had a "little thing" stuck on him. At the time, she wished to "cut it off him" and "plant it on myself."

At about the age of four, she began to fantasize that his penis would be cut off with her "mother's sewing scissors, or chopped up like those carrots" her mother chopped for soup. She reasoned that if her brother didn't have a penis, he wouldn't get all the attention. Judith was sure that intercourse happened by her mother "biting off my father's penis, which then grew back again."

"I wanted my brother dead. I used to lie in bed in the evening when I was four and wish that he didn't have a penis. Or, maybe, I could have his penis on me. That way mommy would pay attention to me."

"Did you believe it was possible?"

"No. I always knew I was just mad at my brother and my mother for her not paying enough attention to me. She thought he was so cute, with that little thing on him."

Deficit: self psychology/psychopathology

Traditional psychoanalysis viewed psychopathology as being the result of psychic conflict resulting in symptom formation. Earlier developmental challenges resulted in conflicts and eventually into infantile neuroses which served as points of fixation in the patient's unconscious mind. Later, when confronted with frustrations in reality, the individual's libidinal energy would "regress" to these fixation points which would then, with this added energy, push forward to overcome the forces of repression. Defense mechanisms would meet these expressive forces resulting in the compromise formations of psychopathology.

The evolving nature of psychoanalytic thinking, particularly with the acceptance of the structural model, led practitioners to think in terms of symptoms being the result of either the traditional "conflicts" or in terms of "deficits." Here, specific ego capacities were either missing or poorly formed, involving thought, affect, volition (motivation), reasoning, language, and memory. Symptoms, in this way, were a result of the ego being in need of new capacities.

Self psychology sees psychopathology not as a result of conflict but rather as a result of deficit, but not in terms of ego deficiencies. Rather, symptoms are a result of the absence of early and current essential selfobject experiences. The "choice of symptom" arises from an admixture of forces. First, there is developmental stage at which the selfobject failure occurred. The normal developmental challenges, unattended, are greatly amplified. Second, the needed selfobject experiences present at that time are now reactivated and with the ensuing threat of fragmentation, overwhelming unconscious negative self appraisal (absence of positive affective coloring of the self) and/or loss of continuity of the self in time, emergency attempts at restoration of the self are initiated. Retreat in the face of depletion, often seen in depression, "circling the horses" and maintaining an oppressive obsessive grip on the self to try to prevent fragmentation, or grandiose/paranoid cognitive constructions/fantasies/delusions to prop up a faltering/failing self are the manifestations of self psychology's psychopathology of deficit. Thus, oral, anal, or oedipal scenario's give color to the emerging psychopathology but as a result of what was and what is missing in terms of support for the self itself. In the here and now, the individual uses "defenses" to ward off this terror of being "re-traumatized" in an experience similar to the original failure. These are occasioned by empathic failures or lapses in current life.[1]

Here we enter the second realm of symptom formation in self psychology—the "vertical split." This is particularly relevant for our understanding of Judith and her "multiple personalities" at this point in the middle phase.

Judith's vertical split

Even though Judith knew these were just fantasies and wishes when she was four, an unfortunate accident led to her becoming convinced that her thoughts had caused problems in the real world: when Judith was four and a quarter, her mother tripped with her brother, breaking his leg.

What had previously been just wishes of harm to her brother became something quite different. Her mother would say that she just didn't know how she could have tripped. But Judith suddenly knew. She knew that her thoughts had made her mother slip, breaking her brother's leg. She felt both guilty and powerful, believing that her thoughts were the cause of her mother's fall.

At this point in her life, believing that her thoughts caused actual harm in the world and feeling guilty about the perceived effects of her angry wishes, Judith developed a four part split in her view of herself.

How does a child develop a split in their psyche? Usually it's the result of physical or emotional trauma. Some part of the self becomes unacceptable to oneself as there is no one available to help the child understand what has happened. Nature abhors a vacuum. It seemed to Judith that her mother's fall and the breaking of her brother's leg were Judith's fault, the result of her angry wishes. The ensuing split seemed to be between the good person she wanted to be and the bad person she believed she was. There was no way to bridge this gap.

As Judith's mirroring selfobject transference to Dr. Steinman took hold, she was enabled to reveal more aspects of her psychic structure without immediate threat of being completely pulled apart. What she revealed was that at the time of these traumas, her emergency solution was to preserve her intact positive coloring of herself through an encapsulation process. This kind of concurrent "anthropomorphization" of these fragmented affect states is not uncommon although they vary in intensity and in levels of differentiation.

As far as Judith was concerned, she was "Judy," four years old in a pink checked dress. "Judy" was pursued by the "Monster," that self who had had all the angry wishes. "Judy" was protected from "the Monster" by "Mother-god." "Mother-god" punished the "Monster" for all the "Monster's" sexual and angry feelings.

> Dr. Steinman reports:
> "How does 'Mother-god' punish the 'Monster'?"

> "'Mother-god' looks after me. She feeds the 'Monster' food to get her to leave me alone. And 'Mother-god' tells the 'Monster' that she's 'such a terrible person'."
>
> "When did 'Mother-god' start telling the 'Monster' that she was 'such a terrible person'?"
>
> "'Mother-god' has always told the 'Monster' that she was 'such a terrible person'. 'Mother-god' is always muttering, 'such a terrible person'."
>
> "When did that start?"
>
> "When my mother fell with my brother and said she didn't know how she could have fallen. 'Mother-god' and the 'Monster' have been with me since."
>
> "Do me a favor, will you? Walk out to the bathroom and let me know what you see in the mirror."
>
> Judith looked at me as if I was the one who was over the edge. "Are you sure?"
>
> "Humor me."
>
> She walked out, returning in about thirty seconds.
>
> "What did you see?"
>
> "Myself. It's a mirror, you know."
>
> "Can you describe yourself?"
>
> "What is wrong with you? Of course I can. I'm four years old, and three feet tall and I'm wearing a pink checked dress."

Here we see the perceptual apparatus hijacked by the forces of affect (Garfield, 2009; Searles, 1979).

> "You know that to me you're in your late twenties, with blonde hair and blue eyes and wearing jeans and a reddish polo shirt."
>
> Intuitively, Dr. Steinman provides a selfobject function of recognition to the patient, one which was painfully missing when her mother fell when she was four years old.

The vertical split: an analogy

Although Chapter Five will explore the vertical split in great depth, it is meaningful to introduce the topic at this point in Judith's treatment to more fully understand her psychosis and her "multiple personalities." Arnold Goldberg, in his book, *Being of Two Minds* (1999) along with colleagues, in the edited collection, *Errant Selves* (2001), deepen the exploration of how vertical splits in consciousness result in the narcissistic behavior disorders. The voyeur, the exhibitionist and other examples of "Jekyll and Hyde" behavior are clarified in terms of the psyche encountering circumstances where untenable affect states are being elicited and the individual shifts into a covert state of patterned behavior which is not unconscious, but rather disavowed. Rather than understanding these processes in terms of a Kleinian defense of "splitting," these shifts are understood by self psychology as emergency self-esteem maintenance measures. The exhibitionist desperately needs to see that she has been "seen" and is no longer invisible. The voyeur desperately needs to avoid the humiliation of feeling diminished or marginalized by the experience of being omniscient. Yet, how does this relate to Judith and her multiple personality?

Here's an analogy. Many years ago, one of us (DG), was walking to his suburban train station to go for his first day of classes at the analytic institute. He had taken this train downtown hundreds of times before. He was a professor of psychiatry at a medical school and had trained several hundred residents in psychiatry. However, walking one block through the park, he began to obsess about whether to walk through the parking lot or cross the park directly. What if he walked through the park and slipped as the grass ended and the pavement by the train station began? His insecurity about the best course to take mounted quickly. Even self reflecting, at this moment, on the ridiculous nature of the anxiety, did not decrease it. He was instantly transported back to the first day of kindergarten when his older sister dropped him off outside the door of the school where he stood for what seemed an eternity before another child's mother asked if he wanted someone to take him in. For the soon-to-be candidate, the end of the grass arrived, he took too big a step, slipped and skinned his elbow and almost cried, all the time partially aware of the absurdity of his experience.

Why is this analogy pertinent to our self psychological understanding of Judith's "multiple personalities"? Early self states in the context of emergency self-esteem needs can become encapsulated and reactivated. Can Judith trust Dr. Steinman to understand the immediacy of her current state and how she needs him to help identify and reintegrate these disparate parts of herself which now threaten her?

> Dr. S: "I think that you're telling us about your psychological life. It sounds to me as if you split yourself up when your mother fell and

broke your brother's leg. It sounds to me as if you felt responsible for her fall and felt blamed and guilty. Not wanting to feel that you were a bad person, you split yourself up into the good 'Judy' and the bad 'Monster', with 'Mother-god' punishing you for all sorts of imagined things."

Instead of sweet reason, my remarks (Dr. Steinman's) were met with disbelief. Judith nearly spat the words at me. "You don't know what you're talking about."

Patients often reject my observations. And that is to be expected. After all, I'm offering a view that may be totally different from what they have believed for years. Yet, this preparatory comment which might have a grain of truth in it, is a first step, a seed upon which a latticework of reality may crystallize as psychotherapy continues.

It is not through argument, but through her gradual understanding of the meaning of delusional phenomena such as "Judy," "Mother-god" and the "Monster," that Judith would reintegrate to one person and heal.

Threats of deficit

Can gentle insight really heal the self? Closer inspection of Dr. Steinman's musing leads us to think "maybe there is more to it." Something happens in the background of successful psychoanalytic processes with patients like Judith. There are ongoing experiences with the analyst wherein a strengthening of the self occurs. A cognitive thought or explanation won't weave together rends in the fabric. They simply aren't "usable" in the context of the threat of deficit. When patients run into trouble, they are bumping into or falling into deficit. The emergency measures established are not easily changed and for good reason. Through her "multiple personalities," Judith offsets the greater threat of "falling into a black hole" or becoming profoundly lost in a disorganized mish-mash of thoughts and inchoate behaviors. In this most distorted of fashions, Judith maintains a continuity of self in multiple forms.

The function of multiple personalities

Perhaps instead of thinking of dissociation as a "distancing" from reality, we might be better served as thinking of it as a distancing from experiencing. Add to that, the idea of a continuum from experiencing to perceiving to observing. Thus, there is a large gap or rend in the intrapsychic fabric. What happens in these spaces in between? They are filled by altered forms of self-esteem/self-image.

These distinctive forms may be, in their own way the efforts of a damaged self to seek out avenues of strength that are not available from real people. The disavowal protects from re-traumatization and the various non-contiguous, non continuous forms that live on inside her, transiently connect her to temporary vitalization. A monster is someone to be reckoned with in an effort to overcome fear and helplessness. A "mother god" is someone who can provide succor and protection to someone who is vulnerable and depleted. A pretty four-year-old girl in a polka dot dress is an assertion of a wholesome and innocent presence.

> Dr. Steinman sought to understand how these multiple figures worked in Judith's internal life.
>
> "Judy" was in thrall to "Mother-god," a vague white robed controlling figure who had existed for as long as "Judy" had. "Judy" had been born when the "Monster" was four. "Mother-god" told Judy what to do in a combination of ways. First she fed "Judy," especially by bottle feeding. This comforted "Judy" and pointed her in the right direction, at least as far as what "Mother-god" wanted "Judy" to do. Secondly, "Mother-god" constantly muttered to herself "such a terrible person." "Judy" was unsure what she had done wrong, but knew she had to do the right thing in order that "Mother-god" would protect her and feed her.
>
> Judith was very confused. We worked on the nature of "Mother-god"—a harsh punitive form of a god-like mother—and "Judy"—the mental embodiment of a regressive, dependent self, feeling the need for protection. As far as Judith was concerned she was primarily "Judy," and related past events from a young child's perspective; at times, if asked, the "Mother-god" self would chime in with additional material.
>
> Dr. Steinman was pretty confused by the whole thing.
>
> "Judith, I don't quite follow," I said, scratching my head in my most Colombo-like way. "Maybe 'Mother-god' can come here and talk to us and tell us how 'Judy', 'Mother-god' and the 'Monster' developed."

Judith didn't appear to respond.

"Hello Doctor" Judith said in a strange, nearly flirtatious, tone early in our next session.

Judith seemed different, livelier and more engaged.

"I'm 'Mother-god'. I've been wanting to talk to you. You know this young girl just can't take care of herself; she needs me to look after her."

As "Mother-god," Judith's tone was condescending and deprecatory. She sighed, pursed her lips and shook her head slowly; she seemed burdened by her perception of her caretaking responsibilities.

"Oh. How so?"

"She is so impossible. There's just no telling what she'll think."

"What do you mean? Let me explain it all to you, Doctor."

"Ok."

"I look after her, poor child. She's so frightened that she caused her mother to fall and broke her brother's leg. She thinks her thoughts caused the fall. I have to look after her."

This was getting eerie. "Mother-god" was beginning to sound more and more like her invention of an internal character who sounded a lot like me (Dr. S.). I thought I'd try to get 'Mother-god's' perspective on Judith's history. "Why does she think she caused her mother to fall?"

Nearly mimicking my speech and tone now, Judith in the guise of a dissociated being, "Mother-god," recounted how Judith got to be who she was.

"Judy' was a precocious little girl; she played piano, read and talked a lot by the age of three. When her mother gave birth to her younger brother, 'Judy' began to resent him for getting all that attention just because he 'had that little thing on him."

She began to wish that his penis would be cut off with her mother's sewing scissors, or chopped up like those carrots her mother chopped for soup. If he didn't have a penis, she thought he wouldn't be so special.

"How do you know all these things?"

"Really! Doctor! I know because I was there. After all, I am 'Mother-god'."

I tried a different tack. "Since we're both on the same side looking after Judith, what else should I know about her?"

"One day, when 'Judy' was four-and-a-quarter, her mother tripped, and broke her little brother's leg. Her mother said she didn't know how she could have fallen, but 'Judy' knew."

"What did she know?"

"Judy knew her angry thoughts about her brother caused her mother to fall."

"Did they?"

"Of course not, Doctor. You and I know that. But 'Judy' felt responsible for her mother's fall, because she wished her brother was gone. She was terrified because she was certain that her thoughts had led to her brother's broken leg. That's where I came in."

"What happened?"

"I showed up; someone had to look after her, poor thing. She was so certain she had done it to her mother."

"How did you look after her?"

"I fed her bottles of milk. I nursed her and comforted her so that she wouldn't feel so bad about what happened to her brother. I soothed her when she was so upset."

"But I thought you said 'such a terrible person' over and over again; how was that looking after her?"

Oozing condescension, "Mother-god" filled me in.

"I did say that, Doctor and I continue to say it. But not to 'Judy'. I say it to the 'Monster'."

"Who's the 'Monster'?"

"The 'Monster' was angry. It was the 'Monster' who wanted her brother gone; it was the 'Monster', not 'Judy', who 'Judy' believed caused her mother's fall. It's the 'Monster' who is 'such a terrible person'."

"Let me get this straight." I was starting to get heated again, this time with a delusional being. "You've terrified Judith all these years for something she didn't do. You scared her so much by saying 'such a terrible person' that this woman in her twenties believes herself not only to be a monster but fools herself even more into seeing herself as 'Judy', a four-year-old girl who is three feet tall and wearing a pink checked dress."

"I guess so, Doctor. I did it for her own good. She felt so guilty about her brother's broken leg. I only wanted to take care of her."

"You took care of her, all right." I was getting a little hot under the collar. I guess I was being protective of Judith in my own way.

"You got Judith to believe she was only four years old, the age at which you emerged and she stayed stuck. You got her to believe she was 'Judy' and that you were nurturing her, while all the time you got her to deny her own growing and developing self which she viewed as an angry monster. Does that sound like being helpful?"

"It was a little confusing to her, Doctor. But I meant well."

I continued the psychodrama that Judith and I were having in the guise of "Mother-god" talking to me.

"I know you tried to look after Judith. But you are the creation of a very upset four-year-old who believed that her thoughts could affect the world. When her mother said she didn't know how she fell with her baby brother, you—the creation of a four-year-old who felt very guilty—jumped right in and helped create a four way split in Judith's being. I know you meant well, but you actually made Judith very confused. I think your work is over."

Her speech slowed. "Mother-god" seemed to comprehend. "Thank you, Doctor. It's been my pleasure to know you. You'll look after her now? I believe she's in good hands."

"I'll look after Judith and help her to understand what this has all been about. That's the best way for her to be strong enough for life. I know you tried to comfort her by getting her to believe you were giving her milk, but in the process, she believed she became three imaginary beings, neglecting the real person she is. My goal is for her to be just one real person."

"I understand, Doctor." Then she said rather coyly. "I wish we could have met in other circumstances."

With that, "Mother-god" was gone.

Extension and deepening of the mirroring selfobject

Judith seemed to waken from a sleep or trance. She appeared to have no knowledge of my conversations with "Mother-god." I explained to her what had happened and the history we had learned from "Mother god."

Judith couldn't comprehend what I was recounting to her. She remained convinced that she was the four-year-old "Judy." This was not surprising, since psychological change leading to clarity often proceeds slowly. But at least I had some information from the horse's mouth to guide my comments.

It was now clear to me (though not to Judith) that the "Monster" was the repository of all of her unacceptable angry thoughts and sensual feelings. Of course, she was explaining all this to me years later and her memories were clearly filtered through time and many layers of experience. The "Monster" was her emergency procedure for disavowing the threat of responsibility, blame and guilt and yet, maintaining it somewhere inside herself as well. Instead of one person, Judith, who wished harm to her brother, quickly turned herself into four; only one, "The Monster" had wished her brother harm.

Like the little kid who raids the refrigerator, then says, "'Piggy' did it, not me," Judith was not responsible in her mind for thoughts or actions. As the years passed, any sexual or aggressive impulse was laid to the door of the "Monster." Here is the manifestation of disavowal.

Fantasy selfobjects

Shane, M. and Shane, E. (1993) and Bacal (1985) have been among the forefront of self psychologists who have elaborated the nature of "fantasy selfobjects" and their role of providing urgent and emergent cohesion to a self threatened by extensive deficit. What we see with Judith and her "multiple personalities" is quite similar. We are, in addition, reminded of the "imaginary friends" that children will so often conjure up in a quest to offset the pain and loss of self due to extreme aloneness and lonliness.

> Dr. Steinman parses this phenomenon further:
> The situation in Judith's mind was something like this. "Judy" and "Mother-god" formed an alliance that had persisted for more than twenty years. "Mother-god" would criticize the "Monster," keeping her submissive, by saying "such a terrible person" to the "Monster." In addition, she was highly self suggestible, and had escaped real and imagined responsibility over the years by believing such a strange and convoluted intrapsychic scenario.
> The question was, why? Why would someone become so deluded? Could the factors we knew about account for her world view? We knew of the mother reaming out the baby bottle, so that epitomized the origin of the tendency not to tolerate frustration.

Her religion emphasized that the thought was as bad as the deed, but only after the age of seven. She had wished harm to her brother, and harm had happened to him. Was that enough to lead to such disordered thinking?

I listened to Judith's thoughts and feelings, personified in these different beings, questioning her necessity for presenting material in this fashion. Could other issues be responsible for the four-way splitting of her sense of self? She was adamant. This was how things really were to her. Even though I saw Judith as one person who believed she was four, Judith saw herself as "Judy" protected by "Mother-god" and pursued by the "Monster." As we went over this material repeatedly; she remained convinced.

"You just don't get it. I'm only four. 'Mother-god' looks after me. We both keep the 'Monster' in check."

"What would happen if you didn't keep the 'Monster' in check?"

"Something terrible, like when my mother fell with my brother."

Dr. Steinman. reflected:

Psychological change may take a long period of time, so I was not disheartened. I knew we were gradually unwinding some of her delusional attitudes and beliefs. With my own certainty about the benefits of intensive psychotherapy I had no doubt that Judith would reintegrate over time.

But first, I had to make certain that Judith stayed alive.

At that point in treatment, I tabled the issue of whether Judith was Judith or "Judy," "Mother-god" and the "Monster," for we had about two months before her birthday, and she had told me that this birthday could be her death day.

"What are your plans for your birthday?"

"What do you mean?"

"You told me that nine months from the time you gave birth to yourself here in the office that you'd decide whether to live or die. I figure you have about two months more to make that decision and wondered what your thoughts were about staying alive or killing yourself."

Judith became furious at me, screaming indignantly. "I hate you, and all your talking about everything. I hoped you had forgotten what I said."

"Why?"

"Because I'm going to kill myself for my birthday."

More precisely, the alliance of "Mother-god" and "Judy" had decided to kill the "Monster." "Mother-god" persisted after our talk within Judith. Somehow, "Mother-god" and "Judy" believed they could exist after they threw the "Monster" off the Golden Gate Bridge.

This was a point at which a lot of psychiatrists might have hospitalized Judith. But I knew we had two months to sort things out and there was so much to make sense of for Judith. I put the hospital on the back burner and explored the situation with her.

Judith talked a great deal about suicide and frequently threatened to cut herself, as she went through this stage of treatment, but she didn't act on these impulses. The old "Mother God" and "Judy" alliance wanted her dead; some other aspect of her wanted to live.

Judith was always punctual, much more so than I. So it was with apprehension that I realized she was late for an appointment.

"Could I be wrong about her ability to get through this suicidal situation?" I mused. "Should I have hospitalized her? Maybe I need to put her back on antipsychotic medicines. I hope it's not too late."

The smiling man's voice

I tried her at home and called her family. No response. In those days before cell phones, there was no easy way to reach her. My ruminations grew as the minutes ticked away. Halfway through the session, the phone rang.

"I'm at the water near the Golden Gate Bridge." Judith sounded distant.

"Are you all right?"

"I'm okay." Her speech was slow and halting.

"That's good. What are you doing there? You're supposed to be here."

"I wanted to kill myself. I wanted to jump in the water." Judith sounded frightened.

"Do you need me to come and get you?"

"No. I'm okay." She seemed to be trying to reassure me.

"Is your car right there?"

"It is."
"Can you make it over here immediately?"
"Uh huh."
"If you can't, I'll come over there."
"No. I can come over right now." She seemed relieved. And so was I when she walked through the door ten minutes later.

"I'm glad you're safe, Judith, but I'm very concerned about you. What you just did is extremely serious. Fortunately you called and finally got here, but this belief in 'Judy' and 'Mother-god' and the 'Monster' is potentially very dangerous. We're going to sit here this evening until you finally understand what's going on. Otherwise it's the hospital or medicines again."

"Okay. But I don't need them."

Hospitalization or medication weren't necessary, however, for Judith seemed to be developing another personality, an internal attitude which was extremely helpful as a counter to the murderous impulses of "Mother-god."

"Mother-god and I wanted to kill the 'Monster' Judy confided.

"Why?"

"She's so hateful. 'Mother-god' always says that the 'Monster' is 'such a terrible person'."

"If the 'Monster' dies, what happens to you?"

"Nothing. 'Mother-god' and I will be very happy together; she'll feed me and look after me."

"You really think you will exist if the 'Monster' were dead?"

"Uh huh."

"As I see it, Judith, you've split yourself up into four beings, three of which are imaginary. As far as I'm concerned, you're singularly Judith in your late twenties and not a four-year-old girl 'Judy' in a pink checked dress with a hovering white robed 'Mother-god' looking after you and protecting you from the 'Monster'. As far as I'm concerned, all of you are just Judith and Judith's creative imagining to escape some painful situation."

"Yeah. That's what he says too."

"Who's he?" Now, I was really taken aback.

"The 'Smiling man's voice'."

"The 'Smiling man'. What's he like?"

"Just what it sounds like. He's a smiling man with a nice voice. He tells me what you tell me."

"How long has he been around?"

"Oh, two or three weeks. Pretty much since I fell asleep in your office and 'Mother-god' had that talk with you."

I was delighted that I had an ally. "So what does the 'Smiling man's voice' think about whether or not you should kill yourself on your birthday?"

"He doesn't want me to kill the 'Monster'; but I wouldn't be killing myself. I'd still be here."

"Ask him if you can kill the 'Monster' without killing yourself."

Judith, viewing herself as the four-year-old "Judy," cogitated for several minutes then said slowly. "He says I'm just one person and that I'd kill 'Mother-god', 'Judy', Judith and the 'Monster'—even the 'Smiling man's voice'—if I killed the 'Monster'." Judith seemed perplexed and puzzled, as if she couldn't quite grasp what she was saying. It was as if a light had just gone on in her head.

"That's exactly how I see it."

I immediately knew that this was a momentous and positive intrapsychic and therapeutic change. In place of the "Bad Devil," Judith developed the "Smiling Man's Voice," an internal positive representation of me which wanted the whole being to live. The "Smiling Man's Voice" aligned with the "Monster" and told the others, as I did, that it was impossible for any aspect of Judith to survive, if she tried to kill herself. The "Smiling Man's Voice" told Judith that "Mother-god" and "Judy" could not survive without the "Monster."

He reiterated what I had been telling her for weeks, describing Judith's trying to run from herself and responsibility by splitting herself up into different imaginary beings. The "Smiling Man's Voice" and I mimicked each other, reality testing about dissociation, one in external reality and the "Smiling Man's Voice" in her internal reality.

Coherence: the influence of the mirroring selfobject

As we spent several weeks of sessions talking about her four internal beings, Judith's suicidal impulses gradually diminished. The internal drive for death decreased. She still talked of jumping from the Golden Gate Bridge, but now it was to butt up against my sailboat and be rescued by me. Instead of feelings of suicidal badness, she had a desire to be fused with me, as her body in the water floated right next to my boat.

By her birthday, as we continued to do intensive psychotherapy focused on her unity as one person with widely disparate feelings, wishes, and thoughts, "Mother-god" disappeared. Judith, with no small assist from the internal and external "Smiling Man's Voice," had decided to live.

Several weeks later, Judith again lay on the floor, writhing around for ten minutes without saying a word. After a few minutes of quiet, she spoke. "I've just given birth to 'Judy'. She's wearing her pink checked dress, she's four years old and three feet tall. And, she's dead."

Why dead? What's that all about? It seemed like a positive development, but I wanted some clarification from Judith.

Judith was quiet for a moment. "I don't need her anymore. I don't need to split myself up and pretend things to myself. I'm just one person."

"From your mouth to god's ear. I hope you'll remember what you've just said."

"I'll try" she said softly, smiling from ear to ear.

Dramatic interchanges like this were par for the course with Judith, and of course, things are not black or white: for several years, during periods of stress, Judith was prone to regress and decompensate, with the upsurge of a belief that she was "Judy" dominated by "Mother-god." But for the time being, she saw herself as one person.

The suicidal crisis had passed. Her birthday came and went with no incident. As usual, however, there was more to the story.

Restoration of the bipolar self in psychosis

Kohut's original idea about the development of the self revolved around the the concept of the "bipolar self." Not to be confused with biological psychiatry's "bipolar affective disorder," the bipolar self spoke to the fact there were two main gateways to a viable self in formation. One involved the development of self-esteem, self-regard and self-love through the experience of being recognized, affirmed, and acknowledged. The second gateway to a stable self involved the experience of being protected, guided, and trusted. If one pathway was blocked or in disrepair, an intact self was still viable if the other venue was open and operative. These were the "mirroring" and "idealizing" selfobject experiences and transferences. As we have noted in Judith's case, for most of the opening and middle phase of the work with Dr. Steinman, it was the "mirroring" selfobject experience that held center stage as Dr. Steinman never lost track of the many different past, present and future aspects of Judith's life. Yet, the kinds of disturbances encountered with psychotic patients almost always implies that there are early and severe deficits in both poles of the bipolar self. And as the "suicidal crisis" morphed into a period of "regression," we can see how the focus of the work shifts to repair of the other side of the selfobject continuum—the idealizing selfobject experience.

Note

1. To the extent that self psychology views narcissism or "ego libido" as the primary source of the psyche's eventual structure and function, symptoms that arise that are not only a result of unconscious processes, but also of narcissistic disturbances in conscious life.

CHAPTER THREE

Repair of the self—Judith

Forward and trailing edge transferences

As mentioned earlier, Marion Tolpin's groundbreaking (2002) elaboration of a transference continuum involved the idea that Kohut's mirroring, idealizing and twinship selfobject experiences lay at the forward edge of growth and development whereas the classic repetition compulsion transferences could be seen to be the re-enactment of the unconscious conflicts of childhood. The understanding of the emergence of symptoms in the course of an established treatment may point to the breakdown or shift in forward edge growth facilitative experiences. This then leads to classical transference phenomena.

> After Judith's "delivery" of the dead four-year-old and her announcement of "integration" into "one" self, there followed a period of some six months of "regression." Judith spent much of her waking hours in fantasies of nursing and sucking. At first it would be a bottle, then a nipple, then a whole breast. Gradually, there were images of penises, penises to suck on, penises to cut off, penises to bite off. These images were accompanied by great fear and apprehension.

"There's one" she said tentatively.

"What?"

"A penis" she whispered as her face contorted and her hands defended her mouth.

"Where?"

"Your shoe."

Soon penises were jumping out of my office plants, my hands as I gestured or the corner of the room. Generally these penises were attacking her mouth. She would abruptly move, as she envisioned an attack by a penis. Gradually snakes began to attack her in her reality, or sinuously slide through the room or coil in the corner. She deconstructed the word "therapist" into two words and started to refer to me as "the rapist."

She had no idea of what any of this might mean. She had once seen a "pink snake" when she was five years old, slithering along the road while with a relative; she couldn't remember whom. With the exception of her little brother, she had never seen a penis as far as she could recall.

"Why do you break down therapist to 'the rapist'? Does this tell us something?" It seemed to me that it did.

"I don't know."

"It's cute and creative to break apart therapist and make it 'the rapist'. But you appear terrified as you describe these penises and snakes slithering around and trying to attack your mouth. There are even penises attacking you from my shoes and hands. Are you transferring something from your past into our therapy situation?"

The nature of empathic failure

No analyst or therapist is capable of perfect continuous empathy. Not understanding, not being able to "read" the patient's mind and being unknowingly on vacation or absent when the patient feels the need for the analyst to be present are all day to day examples of the inevitability of empathic lapse or failure. At the point where Judith is now in a totally new and foreign internal mileu, Dr. Steinman finds himself at a loss. Perhaps, this was a "concordant" (Racker, 1968) countertransference experience as Judith was at a loss as to how to proceed as a "whole" individual. Perhaps, it is in that context that Judith falls back into this current regression.

Judith continues: "I just don't know."

"Are you telling us you were raped?"

Judith was silent for a long few minutes, then said softly, "I just don't know."

The sucking fantasies continued. Some days Judith would report being filled with a white warm fluid. Other days, she recounted fantasies of being a young girl given enemas, and gradually being filled with a whitish fluid. Slowly recollections of her mother giving her enemas surfaced. Through the years, I've learned that it seems best to let the patient arrive at the heart of the matter.

So I listened.

With Dr. Steinman's focused attention, Judith begins to re-aneal and begins to become aware of old memories.

Soon material began to emerge about her grandfather who had committed suicide shortly before Judith turned six. She had some vague memory of his looking after her during kindergarten. In the afternoon, she remembered that her mother would drop her off; grandfather would take her to his workshop. After a few weeks, she recalled that when she was alone in his workshop with him, he asked her if she wanted to be special to him. When she said yes, that she wanted to be special to him, he began to molest her; the molestations continued for a year and a half, in various ways.

She revealed this material anxiously, haltingly, and in fragments, often convinced that what she was bringing up couldn't be true. She remembered that after every molestation episode, he would offer her candy and cookies he kept in a bag. When he offered her sweets, she knew the episode was over, and she could relax.

He swore her to secrecy, saying that this was what made her special to him; she complied with keeping the secret She gradually pieced together that she was not only starved for affection and attention, but terrified of him.

"He used a gun."

"What do you mean?"

"He'd threaten to shoot me if I told. And he'd touch me with it all over my body."

"That must have been awfully scary."

"It was" Judith said with tears of relief as she sobbed.

Here one can understand the need for a "Monster" to scare off those who would terrify us.

After a few minutes, she blurted out, "He said he would kill himself if I ever told anyone. But I never did, or don't think I did. But he killed himself. I must have told."

Here we can also see the need for a wholesome four-year-old who would never hurt anyone, either a little brother or a disturbed grandfather.

For several sessions she wailed about her grandfather, the terror she experienced and the effects of his killing himself. It all made sense to me. She thought that some part of her, the "Monster" must have told people what her grandfather did to her and that was why he had killed himself.

If it were true, the molestation would have deepened the already existing rends in Judith's being, reinforcing the vertical splits within it. Judith would have removed herself from these experiences by pretending to herself that it was the "Monster" who was molested, while "Judy" and "Mother God" were not affected by it. "Mother-god's" repeated "such a terrible person" would apply to the "Monster" who was molested.

Judith had trouble believing these events actually happened, though it all added up. She began vomiting in kindergarten, was taken out of school by her mother and often left in the care of her grandfather. When he committed suicide—with a gun—shortly before she turned six, no one said anything about why he had died.

To cope with her grandfather's molestations, Judith would have dissociated, removing herself psychologically from the traumatic events. In her four-and-a-half-year-old mind, she wouldn't be forced to do sexual things with her grandfather; the "Monster" would be the one in the sexual activities while "Judy" and "Mother-god" stood by, observing.

This intrapsychic scenario of four beings, one real and three imaginary, served to make Judith feel even worse, and more confused than she would have from the repeated molestation alone. When the molestation would end, "Judy" would feed the "Monster" to comfort her, while "Mother-god" would repeat "Such a terrible person" over and over again. What would have been intended by Judith as a means of getting away in her mind from her grandfather's predations led to a disavowed orchestration that left her invisible and at ongoing risk.

As she recovered her early experiences under the attentive eye of Dr. Steinman, she was no longer regressed.

Judith, however, couldn't believe it to be true. "How could that have happened? We were such a nice family. I must be imagining it."

Dr. Steinman noted:

I tried to move Judith to accept the reality of traumatic events which seemed convincing to me.

"It's unusual to hallucinate attacking snakes and penises in my office. This tells us something, probably that this was a re-experiencing today of something that had happened to you in the past. First you're attacked by snakes, symbolic penises. Then penises appear to come out of my body and attack your mouth. I think these current feelings are experiences from the past."

"I just don't know what happened."

"Then you see me as a rapist; why would therapist become the rapist? I believe you're trying to tell us what happened to you in the past."

The protective older man turned out to be her abuser. Perhaps, she unconsciously feared Dr. Steinman might turn out to not be protective as well. The fear of re-traumatization elicits the symptoms that express the concern to Dr. Steinman.

"I don't know where these images and details about my grandfather come from. I just can't accept that he would have done that to me."

"His molesting you would be hard to accept. Unfortunately, it seems likely to me that your grandfather did molest you and that your reaction to the molestation—a pretty common reaction—left you more confused and split into what you viewed as different beings. Hopefully it'll become clearer as we talk."

"I just don't know."

It is generally agreed that it is far better for someone to resolve in their own time, as they become increasingly strong psychologically, the reality or fantasy of their productions. With Judith, such an approach left things open for continued delusional life for several more years.

Even though Judith could work and relate superficially to others, she lived in an altered state. Her internal consciousness was caught up with "Mother-god," "Judy" and "the Monster" and there were others who gradually became apparent as we talked.

During this time, Judith would sit quietly in the office, seemingly in a reverie. Sometimes, she barely talked for the first ten or fifteen minutes.

"Why so quiet today?"

"I dunno."

"You've been like this for weeks, now. Where does your attention go?"

"Nowhere," she prevaricated.

"Come on! I know you're thinking about something." I grew up in a teasing family; perhaps it would work here.

"Can I tell you?"

"Of course."

"You won't think it's weird?"

"Of course not."

"I'm your baby. I live in you. Isn't that weird?" Judith looked puzzled, yet relieved to talk about it.

"No, Not at all. What do you suppose this means?"

"For a long time, I've been in your uterus. I know that's really strange, but I think about it a lot. Hour after hour. I'm not born yet and you don't have a uterus, yet I live in you. Isn't that crazy?"

"It's not crazy at all. It's a psychological experience of closeness, fusion and safety in my fantasized womb. People do that sometimes as a way of feeling comfort and protection as they start to heal; we call it the container of psychotherapy. Many books have been written about it."

Here, in lay words, Dr. Steinman describes the establishment of an early merger self-object experience.

"I see." Instead of the dazed look she often showed, Judith's eyes were clear; her expression thoughtful.

By the next session, however, she was back to her old self. She looked vacant and preoccupied, lost in some type of reverie. She was quiet and internal. I was not surprised for this was to be expected, two steps forward and one step back.

After a pensive while I asked, "What are you thinking about?"

We sat quietly for ten minutes; the silence was peaceful.

"Well, there is something. But it's even weirder." She paused.

"We've talked about quite a few things that seemed strange, Judith; yet they always made sense once we discussed them. Give it a try."

"I have a baby in me. It's a fetus. It's been there for years and years."

"Who's the father?"

Sheepishly, Judith said, "My father. But lately it's you."

"How did that happen?"

"I'm real close to you both."

"A boy or a girl?"

"It's a girl. She's me, me before I was born."

"And she's been there for years?"

"Yeah," Judith responded dreamily. "She's safe there; no one will hurt her."

Themes repeat themselves in psychotherapy, until they are worked through. Psychological issues cry out to be understood and finally resolved.

"Who would hurt her?" I asked gently.

"You know who; my grandfather," she whispered.

"Has the baby been there since your grandfather hurt you?" I led the witness a little, hoping that this time through Judith could finally resolve in her own mind what had happened to her.

"Don't talk about it." Judith's screamed at me as her face scrunched up. Her hand quickly protected her mouth as she recoiled in the chair.

"Why not?"

Judith looked frightened, pointed to her side and whispered softly, "He's right there."

"Who?"

"My grandfather." She was nearly cringing in her chair, pointing off to her right.

"What's he saying?"

Judith cocked her head and thought for a moment. "He says not to tell, that he'll hurt me. He says bad things will happen if I tell. He sounds really mean."

"Does he say anything else?"

Softly. "That I'm special." A smile spread across her face.

"How long has he been there?"

"A long time."

"How long?" I asked, pretty certain of the response.

"Since all those things happened with him."

"I think you mean that your grandfather molested you and threatened to hurt you if you told. Not only did that scare you in your day to day life then, but the impression of what happened with him has been with you ever since, even to the extreme of your believing that he's still here with you, alternately threatening you and telling you that you're special."

"I think so" Judith barely nodded.

"You were traumatized by what he did to you when you were young; once he killed himself, he stayed with you in your mind, scaring you and keeping you confused. You retreated to the baby in you to get to safety, to get away from the delusion of your threatening grandfather. He's gone and can never again threaten you."

Judith seemed to coalesce; her face brightened and the tension diminished. "I see what you mean. I've been trying to protect myself from something that happened long ago. I've been living as if it still went on; but he's long dead." Judith's voice trailed off as she thought about the meaning of what she said.

Understanding and explaining

Kohut's (1984) original formula for "How does analysis cure" involved a two step process: (1) Empathy and (2) Interpretation. The traditional psychoanalytic mechanism of change maintained some place in Kohut's schema in terms of the "explaining."

> Dr. S.: "It seems very likely to me that you were sexually traumatized by your grandfather. But you have great trouble accepting what happened to you. The result is that you're mired in an intermediate world where reality is unclear. Your not accepting the reality of what happened to you leaves you in a delusional world."
>
> "He had a gun." Judith whispered, her lower lip quivering. "He threatened me with it and used to touch me with it, everywhere. He scared me so much. I waited for it to be over, to get the candy. That's when I knew he was finished." Tears streamed down her face as she sobbed uncontrollably.
>
> I sat quietly for several minutes as she cried. I knew intuitively that an accepting silence was the most comforting and least intrusive. As she quieted, I empathized: "I'm sorry; it sounds horrible

for anyone to have to go through what you did. I can imagine how terrifying it was when you were four or five."

"I hated him for what he did to me" she screamed. "I wanted him dead."

"Who can blame you for wanting him dead?"

"I thought I had done something or told someone and that was why he killed himself" she wailed through the tears.

After a few minutes, I commiserated. "It would be a pretty normal feeling to hate someone who did what he did to you. Your confusion over these years makes sense because you thought your thoughts could kill or cause your mother to fall, breaking your brother's leg. You tried to deny who you were from fear of causing harm in the world."

Judith paused for a moment, thoughtfully. "He really did all those things to me." She seemed to have more substance; the angles of her face seemed clearer and strongly delineated. Judith was working through the origin of her psychosis.

Years later, she heard from relatives that her grandfather had been a very bad man. Later still, she heard from another female relative that grandfather had molested her too.

While Judith believed her own delusional constructs, she appeared bland and internally preoccupied. She could be convinced of devils, angels, mother-gods and little girls talking to her with great emotion and force, yet kept it all under wraps. Her intensity had been withdrawn inward; to the outside world, she appeared calm and aloof.

As the origin of her psychosis became clearer to her, Judith became much livelier. She voluntarily focused on a number of internal beings she had believed in and, at times, feared.

From fantasy selfobjects to enlisting helpful others

"There are some more people."

"What do you mean?"

"You know." Judith was playful now. "Just like 'Grandfather'. Other people I see and hear sometimes."

"Tell me."

"I don't know when they started, but they've been around for years and years."

"Who are they?"

"Well, I guess they're all parts of me. But I believed they were real until I understood what 'Grandfather' was all about. Now, I know that I created them." Judith was starting to do some psychotherapeutic work on her own.

"Tell me who they are and what they represent."

"Ok; I'll try. There's 'Jod 1'. That's me at the age of seven, when difficulties started at school. She's confused and stands up and sits down in school. She says, 'Don't tell anybody anything'."

"I also have a 'Jod 2', me at the age of nineteen, haggard and disheveled while being given shock treatment in the hospital. She cries a lot and feels hopeless. I guess she's awfully sad. She's me when I'm really unhappy."

Judith wipes some tears away and soldiers on. "Then there's 'Jud'; he's fourteen and awfully angry at things; I wasn't supposed to be angry at anything. Jud is always telling me to get mad at things, but I try not to."

"Why not?"

"I'm just not supposed to get angry. Only the 'Monster' gets angry and then 'Mother-god' says, 'Such a terrible person'. Besides, 'Grandfather' doesn't want me to be angry. He wants me to be nice. Until a few weeks ago, he used to threaten to kill himself if I said anything."

"'Grandfather' is gone now. I haven't heard anything from him or seen him since I told you a few weeks ago that he was with me, terrifying me, all those years." Judith was clearly relieved as she burst into tears again.

"That's wonderful, Judith." We sat in peaceful contemplation of her changes.

After several minutes, I asked, "Is anyone else there in your mind?"

"There's 'Josie'; she's sixty-five years old and can't do anything for herself. I don't know if she represents my mother or my fears of who I might become, but she scares me. She tells me to give up and let people take care of me in the hospital. I never want to be like her."

Finally, Judith was taking to psychotherapy like a duck takes to water. She was bringing up issues, recognizing conflicts and dealing with psychological material in a new way. With her

'Grandfather' recognized as the hallucinatory residue of past traumatic events, her fears diminished and all the different beings dissolved. Judith was left as one person, Judith.

Follow up

Judith has been off antipsychotic medications for nearly four decades. During this time she has not needed hospitalization, as she uncovered, explored, worked through, and resolved a delusional system that had persisted since childhood. Having given up her delusional beliefs, she has become much more functional professionally and interpersonally, with only occasional, short regressions during periods of stress.

In remembering herself and her history, Judith has seen that life without the delusional shell game can be possible, pleasurable, and rewarding.

Previously she was felt to be an untreatable schizophrenic, needing very high doses of antipsychotic medications and constant supportive care. Through our psychoanalytic psychotherapeutic understanding and exploration of her intrapsychic life, healing and cure have been achieved where confusion, delusion and disorganization had previously held sway.

During a session after she had recovered from those long years of psychosis, Judith made my day, if not the whole year. With a glint in her eye and a forcefulness never seen during all those lost years, she began.

> "I have to tell you what you must know already."
> "What's that?"
> "You've given me my life."
>
> I was about to say something flip like, "That's what therapy does," but stopped before uttering a word. I knew she was right. Then the perfect response arose.
>
> "Thanks, Judith. That means a lot to me. It's been a gift to both of us."

CHAPTER FOUR

The infrastructure of the vertical split

As we saw in the case of Judith, disavowed action can be seen as the patient's way of trying to hold on to a threatened sense of self agency. Behaviors, actions and a variety of different split off states contain vital elements of an unintegrated self. For Judith, the mirroring selfobject experience, as it deepened, allowed for the reintegration of these various psychotic behavioral states. The key concept here is "threatened." Given Judith's experience with her grandfather, her very psychological existence was at stake.

This chapter, through two clinical vignettes, explores in greater depth Kohut's (1971) concept of the vertical split. Interestingly, Sullivan's (1953) identification of "selective inattention" as a security operation within a self system can be seen to foreshadow Kohut's concept of the vertical split. Stern's (1985) research on the development of agency within the infant and the important role of caretaker attunement to the felt consequences of intended action add to the clinical understanding of disavowed motor acts. Here, faulty selfobject experiences result in the development of an in-depth sector of the psyche that remains conscious, yet disavowed. We clearly saw this in Judith's psychopathology.

This chapter, however, explores the vertical split from a different vantage point—how innate talents and aptitudes may be unincorporated into the psyche—thus depriving the patient of essential sources of vitalization.

These types of vertical splits can be seen to be active in both psychosis and in neurosis and psychoanalytic clinicians may better understand how absent selfobject experiences contribute to them. As patient and analyst work together, a stronger sense of self agency can emerge.

History of the concept

Kohut articulated the "vertical split" of disavowal by contrasting it with the "horizontal split" of repression. In *The Analysis of the Self* (1971), Kohut commented that the vertical split is "a specific, chronic structural change …" In this state, he argues,

> the ideational and emotional manifestations of a vertical split in the psyche—in contrast to such *horizontal splits* as those brought about on a deeper level by repression and on a higher level by negation (Freud, 1925)—are correlated to the side-by-side, *conscious existence* of otherwise incompatible psychological attitudes, *in depth*. (Kohut, 1971, pp. 176–177, italics and bold for our own emphasis)

As briefly introduced in Chapter Three, the evolution of Kohut's thinking about the vertical *vs.* horizontal splits arose out of his work with the narcissistic behavior disorders. The sometimes stunning behaviors that label these patients are society's front page material as the shoplifter, the adulterer, the voyeur, exhibitionist, embezzler, and other more subtle variations on the theme. Goldberg (1999), in his classic book, *Being of Two Minds: The Vertical Split in Psychoanalysis and Psychotherapy*, and (2001), in his book, *Errant Selves: A Casebook of Misbehavior*, points to the specific, side by side personality that enact these misdeeds.

This "alternate" personality, the one that is conscious to the patient and yet, sometimes, foreign, is usually cast as first, misbehaving and second, as being driven by a narcissistic need in the deepest sense. There is good reason to disagree with the first idea ("misbehaving"), but very good reason to agree with the second. In both neurosis and psychosis, the vertical split can be seen to exhibit strange actions that not immediately recognizable to the patient as being a part of his "normal" repertoire of intentions.

Unrecognized talents in disavowal

Certain byproducts of the vertical split may not be "misdeeds" but may reveal a different category—one where innate natural talents are seeking expression in an attempt to restore narcissistic equilibrium.

In our two cases below, we explore the loss of sense of agency or the experienced ownership of one's motor actions in neurosis and psychosis. Clinically, this loss of agency can be linked to Sullivan's ideas on selective inattention that foreshadowed aspects of Kohut's vertical split in a self system. Daniel Stern's (1985) work on the emergence of self agency points to an infrastructure of agency as it arises out of motor acts. Knowledge of these processes makes unusual enactments easier to understand as segmented off areas of experience look for a bridge that can unite a divided self.

The case of Jane

Jane, a patient of Dr. Garfield's, was a successful fifty-year-old, married, Lutheran accountant who worked in a large downtown Chicago firm. Her husband, Donald, worked as a high school teacher and spent a good deal of time at home with their three children—a boy and two girls. Jane is a "nice" person, a bit interpersonally awkward but very smart. Her persistent experience was as being "overlooked" at work. She alternated between feeling less talented than the other accountants or that her talents were unrecognized by the senior partners.

She was a junior partner at the time she came for analytic therapy. Her concerns were that she was anxious and she didn't know if anything could be done about it. She had seen several therapists through the years and had a brief analysis which she thought helped a bit. She worried a great deal. Was she a good enough mom? Would she ever be made partner and be "successful"? She worried about saying the "right thing."

Startle

> "In the first interview, as Jane was telling her story of worry and despair, she suddenly jerked from her seat on the couch with her arms a bit outstretched and it appeared that she might launch

herself to her feet directly at me. As it turned out, in this brief moment, she did not actually leave the couch. She did, however, cry out 'uhh!' It was as though she was intentionally trying to catch me unprepared. It reminded me of walking down a hallway at work and having someone jump out on Halloween with their arms outstretched trying to give you a ghostly fright. Indeed, it did give me a startle which immediately subsided as Jane apologized and said that this kind of 'thing' occurred regularly. She was embarrassed some, but not too much, and continued right on with her story of being a worried woman."

Over the course of many weeks, Jane repeated episodes/variations on her "startle thing." Sometimes she would jerk her head back and then sit up straighter and extend her neck upwards immediately after she would call out "uhh!" At other times, both her hands would dart out suddenly in synchrony with her outcry.

Another example of this unusual behavior was where Jane would twist her head and neck up to and stretch out her legs, in an odd way and exhale giving a small quiet sound. She knew this was odd behavior. It happened about once every four or five sessions. She noted that it would occur at work a few times a week as well. She and Donald had friends who were doctors who wondered if she had Huntington's chorea. She didn't think so, but what did Dr. Garfield think?

"I didn't think it was Huntington's. As a physician, I had seen Huntington's many times. Furthermore, she had no family history of Huntington's which has a strong genetic component. Jane didn't have any other choreaform movements and many of these movements were more sudden than choreaform. She had no tics or adventitious motor movements characteristic of Tourette's syndrome or hemiballismis. Furthermore, patient behavior produced by neurological syndromes such as Huntington's, Tourettes, Wilson's or other basal ganglia diseases had never once produced the kind of countertransference experience that I was having with Jane. Although I was embarrassed to admit it, at first I was a bit frightened by the incongruity and then after it happened again once or twice more, I found it annoying. It seemed too early in the treatment to be having a concordant or complimentary countertransference (Racker, 1968). I wondered later if it was a communicative enactment of some sort—a kind of 'concretized' self-state (Stolorow,

Brandschraft & Atwood, 1987). Metaphorically, I wondered if she was trying to get me to think she was a 'jerk' or 'twisted' in some fashion. Jane made no other unusual motor movements. Overall, none of these hypotheses seemed to fit."

Talents

Jane was talented both physically and intellectually. It was a pleasure for Dr. Garfield to hear about what she could do. She became a lot less anxious as she sensed that he was authentically interested and impressed with her knowledge and skill in international tax and in her developing athletic prowess. At the age of fifty, Jane had only started jogging about five years ago and she had built herself up to the point where she had been able to complete her first marathon. Dr. Garfield admired her determination. Donald had panic attacks which interfered with his being able to go out alone. He needed Jane, or one of the children, or a friend to go with him to social events. Jane felt that Donald was "a mess," just like her. It was a "misery loves company" kind of marriage she would report. At times, Donald would resent Jane's running/exercise priority but he also felt enhanced that he had a wife with a great body and great job who was so devoted to him.

Jane understood her motor movements and vocalizations to be part of her "weird quirkiness." She remembered herself as feeling like the "odd one out" even as a child. Her mother, Harriet, had been a difficult woman who was both, intimidating to and solicitous of her. Jane had a younger brother, David, and it seemed that her father was only concerned about David's development and that Jane's mom was responsible for Jane. Harriet was quite bright, intellectually oriented and yet, quite cautious in social situations. There was a distinct paranoid-like, "calamity is just around the corner" flavor to her attitude. Jane knew that her mother was deeply invested in her and at the same time, hovered about her and pointed out any minor imperfection in Jane's physical or social appearance.

For example, as a child, Jane had a beautiful voice and Harriet said Jane's voice was too "loud" and saw that as a flaw in a "world where upward social movement is everything." She would thus insist that Jane practice speaking softly to her, almost in a whisper, while reciting Shakespeare. Interestingly, none of Jane's friends thought she was too loud. There was another undertone to the mother–daughter relationship. It was a hidden competitiveness of the mother toward the daughter. Harriet had been a dancer in her youth. She was constantly having Jane watch her dance and she was constantly berating herself for not being "graceful enough" even in middle age.

Jane's mother was always dealing with a pulled muscle or hamstring. It was essential that Jane not get in her way when she danced. The mother encouraged Jane to do ballet but Jane wanted to run. Harriet felt this was not "elegant." In addition, while playing word games, the mother would not let Jane look up a big word to see if she had spelled it correctly ahead of time. Jane would have to put down the letters and then Harriet would look it up and point out that Jane had spelled it incorrectly. Instead of praising her daughter for a good try, this kind of restriction instilled a sense of anticipatory humiliation and defeat.

The interesting development was that Jane had her successes in private. After a year and a half of therapy, Jane recalled a memory of going over to the next town for the Memorial Day races at the age of ten. She went by herself, signed up and ran the fifty-yard dash and won the first place blue ribbon. When she went home proud and delighted to tell her family, her parents paid no attention. Interestingly, both Jane's mom and dad thought that Jane was "slow" as a child in terms of academics since she didn't learn to read until second grade. When she won the sixth grade math competition, they, once again, paid no attention. Jane wanted to be smart and she wanted to be graceful and be an athlete. One day, during her freshman year of high school, Jane was walking home by the school's ice rink with a friend. Another girlfriend of theirs had just finished ice skating practice. As it turns out, the friend who had been skating wore the same size skate as Jane. Jane asked if she could borrow her skates for a minute and see if she could do a twirl. She had only skated a few times before. She remembered going out there and carving an almost perfect figure eight and on the way back to the edge of the rink she tried a jump and landed it spot on. Her friends were awestruck. Like her parents, Jane paid no attention to it.

The body's movements: conversion and enactment

> We are obliged to take quite another view of the process of repression when we consider the picture of a true conversion hysteria. Here the salient point is that it is possible to bring about a total disappearance of the quota of affect. When this is so, the patient

> displays towards his symptoms what Charcot called "la belle indifference des hysteriques." ... the ideational content of the instinctual representative-and at the same time as a symptom—we have an over-strong innervation (in typical cases, a somatic one, sometimes of a sensory, sometimes of a motor character), either as an excitation or an inhibition. (Freud, 1915, p. 156)

Thus, in his classic paper, "On repression" Freud (1915) discusses the psychical mechanism by which unacceptable ideas are split off from their attendant affective charge and that charge is shunted into the body and manifests as sensory or motor symptoms. The symptom becomes a kind of communication insofar as it has symbolic meaning. Jane's behaviors, along the lines of a classic Freudian view might condense elements of aggression combined with elements of distress. The "startling" and the "stretching" portray just that combination. Given Jane's upbringing, one can imagine that she has been humiliated repeatedly and that she has been "molded into a shape not her own."

Insofar as these movements might be multiply determined and have intrapsychic or interpersonal meaning, the question arises as to whether her abnormal motor movements are a type of acting out or an enactment. In a more recent look at the concept of "enactment," Frayn summarizes:

> Acting out seeks to communicate unconscious urges and important childhood experiences, yet can present as a resistance to insight. Mutual and interacting regressive transferences stimulate acting-out behaviors that have led to the concepts of actualization and enactment. An enactment is an unconscious but interpersonal communication, in which gestures and body language play a unique role. Initially an enactment may include a component of the therapist's reciprocal behavior as a precursor to fuller dynamic understanding and eventual definitive interpretation. (Frayn, 1996, p. 197)

Many psychoanalytic authors have investigated (Jacobs, 1986; McLaughlin, 1987) the concept of enactment over the last twenty years following on Freud's (1914) seminal ideas in "Remembering, repeating and working through." Frayn (1996) has brought some clarity to the history of this concept, "Enactment really describes an interpersonal event whether the therapist enters into the enactment as the frustrator or as the gratifier of an infantile demand" (Frayn, 1996, p. 198).

Ella Freeman Sharpe's (1940) classic paper, "Psychophysical problems revealed in language: An examination of metaphor," also addresses this relationship of instinctual demand, motor control and language. Concurrently, as sphincter control over anus and urethra is being established, the child is acquiring the power of speech, and so an avenue of "outer-ance" present from birth becomes of immense importance. First of all the discharge of feeling tension, when this is no longer relieved by physical discharge, can only take place through speech (p. 203). Here, Jane's split off sector holds the bodily manifestation of the instinctual demand of pent up "holding in" which first comes out as the arm stretching, then the non-specific vocal expression and later, an attempt to stretch into a physical shape that will let words come out. It is a kind of developmental motor line, up and out of the body into speech similar to that which Sharpe describes. The problem with these descriptors is that they don't address the internal structuralization of the patient's psyche in her or his attempt to "keep the endangered" away from the "endangering" (Ogden, 1986, as cited in Gabbard, 1994, p. 44). In that regard, we must again return to the vertical split.

Splitting, repression, and disavowal

The history of splitting as a psychoanalytic concept is vast. Splitting as an activity to deal with the "disagreeable" was addressed by Freud (1940), with respect to fetishism and psychosis. He first viewed it with regard to disturbances in relation to reality. His thought was that the ego splits itself so that there is one part, the normal ego, that stays in line with reality and another part, which, under the influence of the instincts, detaches itself from reality. Melanie Klein (1946) focused much more directly on splitting as a basis for psychic survival as it allowed the infant, in the earliest part of development, to separate good from bad and pleasure from unpleasure so as to preserve positively colored experience and positive self/other representations. These were preserved in separate mental compartments away from the contamination of negative opposites.

Bonnie Litowitz (1998) has detailed an "expanded developmental line for negation." She elucidated the movement from rejection to refusal to expressed nonexistence and, finally, to denial. Starting with Freud's (1925) brief paper on negation and then also moving into Freud's

(1927) subsequent exploration of "Fetishism," Litowitz outlined the psychoanalytic origins of the differences between a "horizontal" and "vertical" split. She carries Freud's first theme, that "... there is no 'no' in the unconscious" (Litowitz, 1998, pp. 122–123) through to the topic of negation.

In contrast to repression, Litowitz follows Freud's second theme (1940) that "the childish ego ... fending off some demand ... is effected by means of disavowal of the perceptions ... Disavowals of this kind occur very often and not only with fetishists" (Litowitz, 1998, p. 124). As we will see below, "disavowal" happens in psychosis as well as neurosis. Finally, Litowitz eloquently points out "Thus, repression represents a horizontal split within the psychic apparatus (between ego and id): *'I know it and I don't know it'* (italics added for emphasis)." In contrast, disavowal represents a vertical split in the ego vis-a-vis the perception of reality: "I see it and I don't see it" (Litowitz, 1998, p. 126). We are reminded of Jane's perfect figure eight.

Selective inattention and the vertical split

Harry Stack Sullivan (1956) proposed that selective inattention was a basic "dynamism" of mental life. This normal mechanism, put simply, involved the separation of attention from awareness. Sullivan gives the normal example of a marksman focusing on a target. As his concentration, or attention, becomes totally absorbed in the task at hand, all other elements of awareness are restricted. Sullivan remarks on sticking a pin in the behind of someone engaged in this type of activity and having absolutely no response until some time later when that concentration/attention could be relaxed.

This kind of separation of attention from awareness arises out of the needs of the self system and Sullivan contends that the same process applies to the mind's response to interpersonal situations:

> Whenever one's feelings of security in relation to another person are at stake, awareness is rather sharply focused on the particular warnings in all things that are happening to us that require action to restore a measure of feeling of security and self-respect. (Sullivan, 1956, p. 40)

In normal people, it is important for certain outside stimuli to be ignored in situations of threat such that the organism can focus on security operations. The "action" to which Sullivan refers involves two things. First, one must restrict awareness to what is relevant in the current situation. Next, one must restrict recall such that relevant past experiences pertain only to the security task at hand. For our purposes, it is significant to note that Sullivan believed that in order "to keep something external to awareness, quite a few of the things that are connected with emotional experience by awareness have to be routed differently" (ibid., p. 41). Event responses that are kept out of awareness are stored or routed into different areas of the self system.

Pathology presents the clinician with a new view on the dynamism of selective inattention. Here, significant events may not be allowed into the attentional window—we return to Jane's perfect figure eight. Also, the amazement of her friend does not get into Jane's own awareness. But, if we accept Sullivan's argument, then where are "those things that are connected with emotional experience" rerouted in Jane? Why can't she recognize that she has done such a terrific thing? To Jane, the fifty-yard dash and the skating maneuvers were simply one time, novel events. They had no meaning. In selective inattention, "everything is novel, it just has no purpose, you might say .... It is the capacity to eternally overlook things ..." (ibid., p. 43).

Importantly, Sullivan asserted that selective inattention was not the activity of some dissociated system, it is an activity of the self. Events which are anxiety provoking which provoke insecurity and uncertainty and helplessness in dealing with significant people evokes the selective inattention dynamism. In other words, we have "one self, but split systems." Here is Kohut's vertical split.

Furthermore, these split systems, according to Sullivan, get elaborated and refined by the natural integrating tendencies of the mind. The private successes had to be ignored and rerouted into a silent, dissociated "in depth" sector of the mind; one which was intimately connected to "loudness" of the voice, "graceful" movements, throwing back the head at the finish line and throwing out of the arms. Here are the traces of motor acts encoded in a vertical split.

Sullivan and Kohut

It could be easily and persuasively argued that Sullivan's "selective inattention" and Kohut's vertical split are, themselves, very far apart. Sullivan's was an "interpersonal" psychoanalysis that believed that a mind only existed in the context of other minds and that pathology was a result of responding to the memory or the anticipation of such other minds. Kohut's theory was, inherently, an "intrapsychic" one with universal and innate attributes facilitated or stymied by important others. Yet, despite this profound difference between what would be called a "relational" and a "one body" psychology, common developmental origins have spawned each theory. Sullivan's ideas on the "self system" embraced the ideas of a balance between "satisfactions" and "security" needs. Kohut's original ideas also balanced libidinal and narcissistic threads. Both can be seen to be derivative of Freud's notions of libidinal and self-preservative instincts or of object libido and ego libido.

Both Sullivan and Kohut viewed the "self" system as being primary and distinct from the "personality." Both viewed the self as having content and also as having "operational" activity related to protecting those contents (Greenberg & Mitchell, 1983). For Sullivan, content referred to beliefs, images, and ideas coming from "reflected appraisals" which the individual retains concerning himself. "Operational" activity referred to activities like "parataxic" distortions or integrations and selective inattention that protected that content. Similarly, Kohut looked at the self as being supraordinate and characterized by having content and process qualities. Its contents consisted of a grandiose, idealizing or twinship pole or arc and its process qualities dealt with cohesion, positive affective coloring or continuity in time (Stolorow & Lachmann, 1980).

In addition, both theorists aimed squarely at pathology being the results of threats to the self. The type of pathology related to (1) the type of content under assault and (2) the type of processing involved in the management of the intense anxiety. Much has been made of the differences between these two self theorists (Kohut, 1971) and yet, given their common origins, common focus and understanding of pathology, there may be much more overlap than one sees at first glance. In fact, many of the most modern self psychology theorists (Orange, Atwood & Stolorow, 1997), find themselves creating deep channels between these once disparate theoretical domains.

Actions of a disavowed other

Goldberg (1999) sheds great light on two aspects of this kind of vertical splitting that compel attention. The first involves the clear delineation of a continuum of ambivalence. He moves from a discussion of normal ambivalence to a categorization of deviant, known, but vertically split off behaviors. These include circumscribed dissociation, narcissistic personality disorders, narcissistic behavior disorders and multiple personality disorders.

The second, perhaps more important, insight of Goldberg's has to do with ownership and agency. In most of us struggling with what choice to make, the:

> short-lived split is resolved by the winning side claiming a victory over the entire person, and the losing side ceasing to clamor for attention and concern. It is only when we begin to see that victory does not always have a worthwhile resolution and that neither side is able to tolerate losing, that we start to delineate a pathology. (Goldberg, 1999, p. 9)

He emphasizes that "the most striking single point is the feeling of difference and alienation, of feeling as though one is split off from a stranger" (ibid., p. 15).

Goldberg (1999) and Goldberg and colleagues (2001) present these pathologies in terms of the disavowed side harboring morally/socially unacceptable behaviors. Yet, as we can see from the neurotic example of Jane above and from the lessons learned from Steve's psychosis, sometimes the disavowed sector actually contains the person's talents and positive attributes. Important sources of self-esteem can remain hidden and "unusable" in this way.

Steve's psychosis

Steve is a thirty-six-year-old divorced Hungarian house painter who was hospitalized for an acute, disorganized, persecutory psychosis. He was intermittently catatonic and he carried a diagnosis of bipolar affective disorder with mood-incongruent psychotic features. He was sometimes medicated with Lithium Carbonate, Tegretol and Haldol but he would go off his medication when he would get into verbal battles with his brother, with whom he lived. Steve lived in his brother's converted garage. To make matters worse, when he and his brother would fight, Steve would use cocaine and almost certainly become manic and paranoid. It was always about money. Ernie, Steve's brother also worked as a housepainter and Steve would assist him, yet, Steve was a talented car mechanic and had, in fact, designed and installed a hydrogen cell powered car. Ernie was singularly unimpressed with Steve's car and furthermore, Ernie's wife, Angela, was constantly angry with Steve for not contributing more money for rent and food.

Steve was the younger of the two brothers and the household the boys grew up in was violent and chaotic. Their mother was an alcoholic who felt sorry for herself and insisted that the boys wait on her. Their father was also an alcoholic who was intermittently violent toward the mother and the boys had to insert themselves to protect her. They found themselves taking bad beatings on a regular basis. Ernie was a mediocre student but Steve always got straight A's. Interestingly, on admission to the psychiatric unit, Ernie and Angela had not known that Steve was a good student as a child. It was not important in the household. Ernie was fifteen and Steve was nine when the father left and both boys had to find odd jobs to help their mother out who worked part-time as a house cleaner. Ernie soon got a job at a video store and Steve would assist him until the owner finally hired Steve on a part-time basis as well.

During his admission, Steve was quiet in the group therapy sessions, but in the individual psychotherapy sessions, he would openly discuss his cocaine issue and the fact that he could probably contribute more money for rent. He mentioned that he was good with cars. In an odd fashion, in the middle of a session, Steve would shoot his hand straight up in the air. He would then bring it down. Given the fact that he tapped his foot a lot and was fidgety, one wondered if this strange motor act was part of his psychosis. Perhaps it was a perseverative, frontal lobe stereotypy, characteristic of catatonia.

Steve went along with the standard dual diagnosis ward routine and was to be released in a few days. During one session, when asked about the cars he worked on. Steve said that he knew he should be spending more time helping Ernie with the house painting. His hand shot up again. In words, Steve sounded like a guilty child. Yet, the hand shooting up had a curious effect on the therapist. The countertransference reaction to this motor act was one of affectionate curiosity. Steve came off like an excited nine-year-old raising his hand in class to answer a question. When asked about the hydrogen-powered car, Steve, for the first time, went into a clear and lengthy exegesis about the physics of the hydrogen fuel cell. Dr. Garfield, having recently read something in Newsweek about hydrogen fuel cells, was amazed. He encouraged

Steve to say more about this technology, it was soon discovered that this man was a virtual storehouse of engineering knowledge. Ernie and Angela knew nothing about Steve's knowledge in these areas.

Stern's observation of infancy: self-agency

Stern's (1985) foundational work, *The Interpersonal World of the Infant*, provides deep insights into the relationship between motor acts and the infrastructure of agency. The vertical split, wherein the sense of agency is altered, may be better understood in this light. Based on infant observation research, Stern hypothesizes that "self-agency" or that sense of being the author of one's own actions and the non-author of the actions of others is based on the assimilation of three separate developmental, motor-oriented, tasks. These three experiences are: (1) having volition (e.g., having a sense of intention); (2) having control over self-generated action, (e.g., your arm is going where you want it to go) and (3) experiencing the expected consequences of one's actions (e.g., when you close your eyes, it gets dark or when your thumb goes in your mouth, your thumb feels your tongue and your mouth and tongue feel your thumb and you get an additional feeling of comfort).

These three mechanisms are, in essence, a "before, during and after any given motor act." Volition, Stern notes, requires a motor plan executed by muscle groups. That motor plan lives in mental registration which is usually out of awareness. Neuroscience research (Libet, Freeman & Sutherland, 1999) supports the view that volition, via a "readiness potential" is out of awareness.

Stern notes that one becomes aware of the existence of a motor plan when it misfires or mismatches for example, your thumb hits your eye instead of going into your mouth. Volition involves expectation. We expect our motor equipment to do what we have planned whether it be our eyes, hands, or feet. It is important to note that even when we are unaware of our motor plan, its very presence allows for a sense of volition or will which makes actions seem to belong to us and to be "self-acts."

With respect to our investigation of the vertical split in the clinical situation, one might ask: is the patient absent a sense of volition? The answer is "probably not." Stern notes that without a sense of volition, one would experience one's actions as being like what a puppet would feel like … it would be as if one's motor actions were controlled by another directing force. This is seen in persecutory delusions of influence. Again, cognitive neuroscientists have confirmed this sense of alienation with respect to volition in the "alien hand syndrome" (Spence & Frith, 1999). In patients with a vertical split, after the fact, whether it be a case of misbehavior, or as in the cases of Jane and Steve above, cases of unrecognized superior behavior, the patient does actively recognize that the motor behaviors generated belonged to her or him.

The second feature of self-agency that Stern describes is one of self-governance. This occurs during the motor act and involves proprioception. Here, the muscle groups involved in carrying out the action give the individual feedback such that implementation of the motor plan can be self-corrected along the way. This is sensory information about the whereabouts of the thumb or arm or feet in time and space.

Finally, Stern describes a category of situation where there is no volition and no proprioceptive input to the action. An example here might be getting hit in the stomach by one's brother. There is a felt consequence to the action, but no proprioceptive experience during the action. This is what would be experienced as an "other willed action of the other." These types of combinations of volition and proprioception help develop the sense of authorship of action. "I did not will it and I did not govern it but I sure did feel it."

This third and final component of the development of agency is knowledge about the consequences of actions. For all self-initiated and self-governed actions of the self—for example, I put my thumb into my mouth—there is a felt consequence. My thumb feels a wet rugated tongue, and my mouth will feel the contour, texture, and taste of my thumb.

Owned motor actions have a high degree of felt consistency. Each time you vocalize, you feel a unique resonance sensation pattern from your neck, chest, and skull. Self-self actions have a very high degree of invariance. Every time you close your eyes, your world goes dark. The total combination of volition, proprioception and "felt consequences of action" define the infrastructure of self-agency.

From this final component of Stern's, causal structures concerning agency evolve. Temporal and sensory relations between events play a role here. For example, as a baby, if you suck and suck, harder and harder on your mother's nipple, then it will produce more and more milk which you will then feel in your mouth and stomach. This is also a very high probability event. It is at this point that volition and proprioception depend on environmental conditions to cement the felt consequence of the action and thus, "seal the experience of self-agency."

It is in this third component of self-agency that self psychology's concept of the selfobject comes into sharp relief. Kohut's famous reference to the selfobject is that the object is not experienced as different than the self. In fact, he uses the analogy of the selfobject as being like the control the patient expects over his own body and mind (p. 27). It does what the individual expects it to do. The selfobject function is further defined by Goldberg (1995) in terms of its reliability and dependability akin to Stern's requirement for a high degree of predictability in the felt consequences of self-willed, self-governed motor actions.

Feeling you feeling me: a brief foray into the structure of the selfobject

After Kohut's introduction of the selfobject notion in *The Analysis of The Self* (1971), there have been many refinements and expansions to the definition (Stolorow & Lachmann, 1980; Stolorow & Soccharides, 1987; Wolf, 1988). In essence, these elaborations have focused on the function of the selfobject in providing cohesion, positive affective coloring and a sense of continuity in time to the self. A variety of essential selfobject experiences have been detailed such as vitalizing and adversarial ones. The way in which the selfobject "regulates" emerging affects has also been extensively explored.

There has been a general reluctance to get too mechanistic or specific with respect to the structure of the selfobject for fear of taking a clinically useful metaphor and reifying it to an "experience distant" status. Since "experience-nearness" is the hallmark of what distinguishes the clinical theory of self psychology from the other schools of psychoanalysis, a focus on structure might then become distasteful. Yet, perhaps, we can think of the selfobject as a structure without turning it into an "experience distant" thing. Think of it as a link or as a bridge between two parts of "myself." In the experience of agency, there is "intention" or will. Then there is the experience of "body self in motion" and finally, there is the experience of "predictably feeling the consequences of one's own actions."

How does a selfobject experience materialize? As a baby, there is no distinguishing between the satisfaction of the felt sucking of the thumb by the mouth and the satisfaction of mother's voice and hand when, after the burp, the highly predictable pat of her hand on the back mixes with the highly predictable rubbing of the back by her hand and the ever so predictable sigh of satisfaction in her voice which mixes in with the resonance of the burp in the chest wall which mixes together with the contented satisfaction from feeling the rubbing of the back.

In other words, "I become aware of what I am feeling as I feel you feeling me. When I feel you feeling me, then I am feeling me through you. You are the bridge or link between two different parts of me." Here, the active self is connected up with the passive experiencing self. This is closely related to the old concept of narcissism "passing through the object." In the initial identification of and hooking up of one part of the body-mind-self with another part, the selfobject is that seamless bridge or link.

Is disavowal a missing link?

With no felt consequences to volition and proprioception, the stamp of self-agency is absent and volition and proprioception remain unacknowledged. In both Jane's neurosis and in Steve's psychosis, an "in depth" sector of psyche remains split off, only to be channeled and reactivated by certain precipitated need states. These vertically split off arenas manifest themselves as either simple or complex, disconnected, motor sequences that seem foreign to the patient.

Let's walk this down this road a bit further. Let's assume that based on Stern's anatomy of agency, the infant grows into the child. In a highly chaotic family like Steve's, the only highly predictable felt consequences of Steve's actions may have to do with an unconscious and conscious urge to protect his mother (volition), inserting himself in between his mother and his father (proprioception) and taking a beating (felt consequences of his actions). His mother's love, gratitude and loyalty blend into the unique stamp of ownership that Steve experiences with respect to his own sense of agency. Any felt consequences Steve might find from the non-shared environment in terms of his talents and interest that he has in school are consistently interrupted by his problems with attendance.

The proprioceptive feedback of writing or speaking the answers may indeed take place. Yet, does Steve feel the consequences of his talent? In the absence of a highly predictable felt consequence to his knowing things, Steve's intelligence goes unnoticed. A sector of his psyche which is only activated by misrepresentations of his competence sits side by side with the sweet, sometimes psychotic, cocaine abusing slacker. There is no acknowledgement of the hydrogen fuel cell. There is no link within him between his actions on this energy source and the potential experience of being vitalized by his own initiative. There is no selfobject bridge and Steve is left with a split off, disavowed set of motor acts which he does not experience as being of his own making.

The loss of self-agency

How can we think about the experience of agency? One might productively address this question by looking at the cluster of everyday words with which we characterize this knowledge. What is fascinating about this group of words that manifest elements of agency is that they neatly fall into Stern's three step process of (1) volition, (2) proprioception and (3) felt consequences of motor actions. The volition words include initiative, planning, authoring, proposing, directing, and mapping out. The proprioception words include calibrating, fine-tuning, correcting, revising, editing, and checking. Finally, the "felt consequences of actions" words include judging, assessing, concluding, and appraising.

Thus, rather than having a split between the "active self" and the "experiencing self" as is so often referenced in clinical reports, we can begin to see a continuum in the experience of self-agency based on Stern's observations of the development of a core self in infancy. Furthermore, we can begin to see how such a continuum may result in a divided self wherein specific sets of actions, even talents and skills, are disavowed as they have never taken on the "stamp" of self-agency. The sense of agency is imprinted via key selfobject experiences which are deficient in the vertically split patient. Just as a "needy" or "devitalized and unseen" self may reappear in the binge eater and exhibitionist, so too an "athletic" or "academic" self may segment off into "muscle stretcher" or "hand raiser" given a lack of selfobject responsiveness.

Pathological accommodation and self psychology

Clinically, both Jane and Steve's neurotic and psychotic segmented off behaviors could be seen as pathological accommodation made on the foundation of maintaining vital object ties. In order to maintain important relationships to and obtain essential attention from parents, the child must give up certain fundamental needs. The adaptive strategy then becomes a "pathological accommodation." The clinical vignettes of both Jane and Steve allude to several of these concerns. A deeper examination of the pathological accommodation notion uncovers the question of whether such divisions reveal the presence of a "true self/false self" construct as Winnicott (1960) elaborated or whether the Sullivan/Kohut formula of side-by-side experience is more parsimonious from a clinical point of view.

Abramovitz (1995), in her article "Killing the needy self: Women professionals and suicide" (A critique of Winnicott's false self theory), notes:

> Winnicott's ideas are compelling because they accurately describe how a self-organization splits into two parts if the child is pressured to comply with parental narcissistic needs in the service of attachment. They are also evocative, because the term "false self" resonates for people who suffer from the experience of forcing themselves into a life time of contrived accommodation. The visual metaphor of the true self/false self is one of a kernel of truth contained within an adaptive but false shell. (Abramovitz, 1995, p. 178)

Abramovitz asserts that both sectors of a divided self are true and that the split represents the presence of compensatory structure. It is a venue for sustaining the self. According to Kohut (1977), "rather than merely covering a defect in the self, it compensates for this defect" (Abramovitz, 1995, p. 182). One can actually borrow from Sullivan here and consider this split to be the result of "selective attention" of the parents resulting in "selective inattention" in the patient, due to the parents' narcissistic needs or fears.

On the child's side, as Kohut notes, "a self that had been threatened in its cohesion and functioning in one sector has managed to survive by shifting its psychological point of gravity toward another one." (Kohut, 1977, p. 83). Abramovitz concludes the "sector that received the most responsiveness is consciously identified with as 'me'" (p. 183). Now we have the final link in the experience of agency in Stern's continuum. The very highly predictable felt experience of Jane and Steve—each feeling her or his parents feeling her/him in the specific sector of the loyal and incompetent child; each finding the safety of an idealized selfobject experience that sealed the accommodation on one side and the disavowal on the other.

PART II

IDEALIZING

CHAPTER FIVE

Rachel—in need of an internal safe haven

Rachel was a short, wan, twenty-year-old young woman with blonde hair over her face, when Dr. Steinman first saw her on the psychiatry ward, after her third hospitalization in eight months for serious suicide attempts, self mutilation and psychotic behavior. As she had been after the other suicide attempts, she was withdrawn and hallucinating; she looked blank, her attention on inward preoccupations.

On two previous occasions, she had overdosed; this time she had been found, dazed and confused, wandering on the Golden Gate Bridge. There were reddish lines on her forearms from cutting at herself with a safety pin.

>Dr. Steinman:
>
>Rachel didn't particularly want to talk to me, but I had been called in to see her since she was on such a downhill, negative course. Her family was concerned that they might lose their daughter during one of these psychotic and suicidal episodes.
>
>Initially, Rachel was mute as I sat quietly with her. Gradually, she talked reluctantly, still immersed in whatever she was seeing and hearing. In response to questions, I learned that she was the

eldest of two in a business family, her brother sixteen months younger and twin brothers five years younger. Her father was seen as authoritarian and rigid, her mother as inhibited and too tolerant of her father's "tyrannical behaviour."

"You seem to be focused on something internally; if you are, can you tell me what it is?"

To me, she appeared to be hallucinating. Looking intently off into space in a preoccupied way. Rachel couldn't respond verbally, but was clearly very upset and moved to the corner of the room, where she cowered like a bullied child. I put her on antipsychotics and kept her in the hospital for several weeks as we tried to talk and then tried to work with her as an outpatient while she lived in a halfway house. Of course, Rachel was hallucinating then and outside the hospital, even on high does of antipsychotics; she just couldn't talk about it initially.

At this point Rachel was very upset and moved to the corner of the room, where she cowered like a bullied little child.

Engaging affects

It is with a gentle approach that Dr. Steinman intuitively engages this woman whose self is under threat. She is open to his attempt to be of some help. She has a cooperative nature here. But she is scared. Make no mistake about it—fear is in the air. Engaging the affect of fear requires a soft touch and Dr. Steinman adopts that attitude with her.

Even at the very onset of treatment, the self psychological psychoanalyst pays particular attention to the patient's affects knowing that as blood is to the body, affects are to the self. Tuning into their range and intensity, their contour and their movement is essential to the restoration of the self.

Thirty years later, Rachel described her first awareness of the voice in a way she couldn't begin to articulate at the time.

> "This realization (that there was a voice telling me what to do) didn't come until several months after I started therapy with you. I was driving on the highway and I had to pull over because I was shouting out loud at myself, 'You should kill yourself!' over and over. That was the moment when I realized that something abnormal was going on. Until then, I hadn't noticed that there was

anything unusual about having that kind of ongoing conversation, let alone a conversation that was so unilaterally vicious. So there was some shock in noticing what had been going on for a long time."

Before coming to San Francisco, Rachel had been attending a prestigious university in the Midwest, but she had dropped out because she couldn't handle her increasing anxiety and panic about meeting her own very high standards for academic performance. She believed her "job" in the family was to achieve perfection in school. Deciding to kill herself in a few days was the only way she could get a break from the anxiety: if she were dead, school would no longer matter.

Rachel had had several boyfriends in high school; she had limited sexual activity to making out because she had no intention of becoming pregnant. At the end of her second semester of college, she spent one night with a boy she liked, but didn't enjoy the sexual experience, which she stopped short of intercourse. This made her think that she might be a lesbian, and she decided to move to San Francisco to find out whether that was true. She had not been sexually involved with anyone, however, since arriving in San Francisco.

Rachel enrolled in a new school in San Francisco. It was, however, no better for her, as the panics continued. In the new school, she became more confused as the voice urged her to kill herself whenever she had assignments due. Any attempt at school work would terrify her, since she felt she had nowhere to go but down.

A few months later, a man sexually assaulted her at knifepoint and talked about wanting to kill her. Rachel was terrified, but pulled herself together enough to talk him into letting her go. She was physically safe, but felt defiled and hated men. The next day, filled with rage and self-hatred, she burned her arm.

Disintegration: agency under threat

We tried to understand the origin of her controlling voice. Rachel had kept a diary for years and, when she looked back through her diaries, it became clear that she began to speak to herself in the second person, as "you," in the eighth grade.

In high school, an internal harsh female voice arose that told her she wouldn't pass tests, with the result that she procrastinated until the last minute. In college, this mode of dealing with pressure persisted and increased, with great panic around tests and critical internal negative statements to the effect that: "You'll never pass. You're a failure!" Again, Rachel talked to herself in the second person.

After the sexual episode at college, the voice began to criticize her for her sexuality, telling her that she was a terrible person for any type of sexual feelings. When she discovered masturbation in college, the voice became insistently more negative Rachel couldn't talk about why she cut herself. She was just upset.

I asked how she felt, but she couldn't articulate either her feelings or whatever was going on psychologically. She couldn't even talk about guilt, her emotional state being so fragile and intense. I wondered aloud if there could be any relationship between her suicidal behaviour and self-mutilation on the one hand and her sexuality or feelings about her sexuality on the other. She thought not. She had no idea why she was terrified of sexual involvement, since there was no recollection of any sexual trauma. (Years after ending our work, in another psychotherapy, she came to the realisation that her father had sexually abused her when she was a child.) The voice gained increasing power and control over Rachel, sharply castigating her as "nothing," "fraudulent" and "disgusting." Hurting herself seemed to decrease the tension and agitation brought on by the critical, punitive voice.

Shortly after the assault, while sitting in a session with me, Rachel suddenly went blank; her gaze became fixed and she appeared to be responding to something internal. My attempts to get her to talk were of no avail.

Abruptly, Rachel stood up and dramatically raced out the door, shouting at me that she was going to kill herself. Quick as I could—not so quick any longer—I followed her in a Keystone cops routine, chasing her for several blocks until she let me catch her. For her safety, we continued our "outing"; our destination this time was the hospital psychiatry ward.

The green shoots of an idealizing selfobject engagement

"… until she let me catch her." This tiny observation parallels the first "green shoots of trees and grass" that rise to meet the onset of Spring.

What we speak to in this metaphor is the inner inclination, still alive although previously dormant, to reach emotional nutrients that will revitalize a frozen or beaten down self. These are the "tendrils of health" that Tolpin (2002) alludes to in her "forward edge transferences"—the beginnings of an idealizing selfobject experience. Rachel wants to be "caught" because she needs what she senses Dr. Steinman might have to offer. How to secure it?

> Dr. Steinman continues:
> "In the hospital again, Rachel told me that the voice had been getting stronger, urging her to kill herself. After ten days, on higher amounts of medicine and an exploration of her suicidal thoughts and actions and the delusion of the power that the voice had over her, Rachel stabilized. This time though, she refused to go to the half-way house she had stayed in after her previous hospitalization. The laws of California being what they are, and with Rachel saying she was no longer suicidal, there was no option but for her to return to the apartment she shared with roommates."

She engaged with Dr. Steinman in intensive psychotherapy. Within several weeks, she started a new job, where she functioned quite well.

> "Most of our time was spent on the pressure and distress she felt at the job; and since she appeared to be worsening, antipsychotic medicines were increased to try to diminish her intense panic. I was worried about her and insisted she call me over the weekend to let me know how she was doing. The next day, Saturday, Rachel called to check in from her apartment. She was cagy and evasive. I pushed to find out how she really was. It soon became clear that Rachel was trying to hide her intention of killing herself. I continued trying to talk with her, trying to provide some safety and protection for her over the telephone, but to no avail.
> "The voice is in control. I hate you for trying to keep me from killing myself. Now there is nothing you can do to keep me from my death!" she fairly screamed at me. As I tried to calm her and keep her on the phone while my wife called the police on another line, Rachel became increasingly furious at me, her parents, and herself. In a bombastic, stentorian tone, she yelled, "The voice has

won, the voice has won!" and raced out of the apartment, leaving the phone off the hook.

"I shouted into the phone for a few minutes and finally roused her roommates and urged them to search the apartment for clues. Just as the police arrived, the roommates found a series of suicide notes to me, her parents and her friends.

Piecing together the information in all the suicide notes, it became apparent that Rachel planned to jump off the Golden Gate Bridge the next afternoon at 4pm. Although there was an all-points bulletin out for Rachel and the police at the Bridge had been alerted about her intentions, I still felt the situation was chancy.

Tricky and angry as the voice aspect of Rachel was, there was no guarantee she'd go to the Golden Gate Bridge at all; she might try suicide by another means. Yet she had said she was going there. I called the San Francisco police, the state police and the Golden Gate Bridge police to alert them to Rachel's plan, but didn't feel comfortable with that alone. It's so easy for someone to slip through the cracks in a life-or-death situation like this was becoming. I figured I needed some additional backup; now, where to find it?

Of course; the solution became clear to me. I called her parents, explained the situation to them and recommended that they immediately go to the southern entrance of the bridge on the Bay side and wait for their daughter. If she showed up, they should corral her as quickly as possible and then yell for the police or Bridge Patrol to take her to the hospital. They quickly and apprehensively agreed.

I had thought that both parents would go to the bridge together, but they thought differently. In those pre-cell phone days, the father stayed home to monitor the situation and maybe get some phone calls about her.

By 8:30pm that evening, Rachel's mother was on the bridge, standing guard. Sure enough, the following morning at 9am, not 4 pm, Rachel walked onto the bridge, past the toll booths, unnoticed by any police presence. As I had suspected, Rachel didn't stick to the timing of her suicide plan. Having inadvertently given away her plan during the check-in call, Rachel abandoned the specifics of it. After spending the night outdoors, she started walking to the bridge in the morning—there was no reason to wait once it was light. Imagine Rachel's surprise when, after another hundred feet onto the Bridge, her mother grabbed her and marched her over to the police. Rachel was so dissociated that she made no response and couldn't even speak to her mother. Though mute at the time, Rachel eventually told me, she was certainly grateful to her mother later on."

Getting a grip on herself

As discussed earlier in this book, one of the hallmarks of an idealizing selfobject experience is feeling like one is safe "under the wing" of a powerful other figure; that one is "a part of" this larger unit. In small but emerging ways, Rachel has the opportunity to piece this experience together. Once it takes hold, an idealizing selfobject experience can markedly decrease the patient's anxiety as a soothing, reassuring internal experience spreads.

During the subsequent hospitalization, her fifth, a more detailed exploration was made of the compelling voice and her psychotic and suicidal regressions. It was a slow process.

Initially, Rachel was near catatonic for several days, trembling, often mute, despairing and non-communicative for the better part of sessions. Suicidal intent remained strong; guilt about anything sexual continued to be intense. Rachel would run out of the hospital psychotherapy office and scratch herself, while the voices told her that she was horrible and disgusting for sexual thoughts. The voice threatened her with harm.

First, as we explored the voice, some attempt was made to help Rachel understand that the voice might represent her guilt about sexuality.

> Dr. Steinman:
> "Her intrapsychic conflict was projected outside of herself in the form of a harsh, berating voice instead of the internal superego attitudes most of us have. I reality tested that the voice represented her own thoughts and guilt, not the presence of an external, supernatural voice of an authority. The best that we could come up with was that the voice sounded like her father due to Rachel's conflicts about right and wrong, put into the concretized form of her father's voice, criticizing her and placed outside herself. During our work together she gradually recognized that the voice came from her and represented her view of some of her father's values.

> Secondly, the origin of guilt about sex was discussed. Rachel stated: 'My mother doesn't want me to be sexual; my father doesn't either'. Rachel had no idea why her mother wouldn't want her to be sexual. I wondered if she wanted us to talk with them about sexuality, but Rachel refused. She had no awareness then of any previous sexual trauma.
>
> Thirdly, the origin of guilt about her anger at her parents, her father in particular, was discussed. Some family sessions were held in the hospital, in which Rachel raged at her father, then succumbed to overwhelming guilt, withdrawal, self-loathing and attempts to harm herself. She had no idea why she punished herself for her anger at her father. This theme of anger, then punishment for her anger, played out again and again."

Rachel had been medicated on reasonably high doses of antipsychotics. Dr. Steinman's experience with the intensity of her voice and her dramatic suicidal urges and punitive cutting and burning, led him to the conclusion that the best that could be done was a gradual psychotherapy, slowly decreasing her antipsychotic medicines as Rachel gained control over the conflicted areas.

In the best of all therapeutic worlds, Rachel would have stayed in the hospital for a long period of time. The best that could be done, however, was a six week hospitalization, with discharge, to a half-way house.

Unsurprisingly, Rachel refused to stay in the half-way house after being there a week. She had again become suicidal, regressing to the voice, even on higher doses of antipsychotic medicines.

The family couldn't fund the hospital forever; what could be done? Was this bright, creative—although psychotic—young woman to go the route of repeated hospitalizations or custodial care in a locked facility? It just didn't make sense.

> Dr. Steinman:
>
> "The solution to our dilemma was where it was the previous time. I talked with the parents, explained the situation to them and got them to agree to take her home. Both parents were highly motivated and concerned about their daughter; although they were not terribly sophisticated psychologically, they were ready to work with me to provide an understanding, caring environment in which their daughter was not likely to seriously harm herself.

Rachel began dynamic psychotherapy with me three times weekly. Over the next five months, with occasional meetings and regular phone calls with the parents, she was able to titrate down and stop the antipsychotic medication. It was only used thereafter during a few life threatening crises, perhaps ten times over the next year and a half of her treatment with me, as Rachel worked through and integrated her harsh superego conflicts which been reified as the delusion of a berating voice outside of herself."

Enlistment: a sign of a stronger self

Notice that Rachel was not the only one who needed reassurance and assistance. Dr. Steinman, as noted above in the episode of the Golden Gate bridge, quickly realized that he needed help with Rachel (needed to find some anti-anxiety, unifying, team of his own), and he enlisted Rachel's parents—not only to offset the repeated suicide attempts but now to provide an environment where Rachel could work with him in their psychotherapy. This "concordant" countertransference (Racker, 1968) signaled the continuation of the engagement process that Rachel had initiated with Dr. Steinman.

Dr. Steinman continues:

"The main thrust of therapy was to explore the primitive superego conflicts. Obviously, in living at home, there was a sense of Rachel's being cared for and nurtured, with many fantasies of being a little girl and of retreat to the womb. I understood these fantasies to be yearnings to be free of conflict, close to her mother and, further, as a desire to escape guilt about sexual and angry feelings.

During these first five months, while she was on antipsychotic medication, Rachel had many episodes of withdrawal, tremendous outpourings of guilt and self-vilification as well as exacerbations of the voice, chastising her and urging her to suicide. Her guilt appeared to be about several things. She would rage at her father for the controlling things he did, then feel she was terrible for reacting and being so mad at him. In addition, she felt very uncomfortable about any sexual feelings and fantasies she had, berating herself for them. When either anger or sexual feeling came up, she would be likely to bang her head against the wall, cut, or hit her left arm and hand and retreat into rocking in an attempt to comfort herself.

Gradually, her self-mutilation of the left hand was understood psychodynamically as guilt about sexuality and masturbating. She retreated into hallucinations telling her she was bad when her guilt about anger and sexuality became too powerful."

Sexualization of the deficit

From the viewpoint of self psychology, Rachel was struggling with a deficit wherein she was absent the internal means by which to soothe or comfort herself or feel confident or proud of her own being in the world. Although the manifest content of her communications in the therapy revolved around the discomfort of her sexuality, the engine of her distress was the deficit in her self cohesion. Recall that Stolorow and Lachmann (1980) detailed the three main functions of the selfobject as being: (1) providing an internal sense of positive mood; (2) providing an internal sense of cohesion and (3) providing an internal sense of continuity in time. Here, Rachel is most in need of an internal experience where she can experience a sense of cohesion and of being one integrated self; also, she rarely experienced a positive coloring of her day to day mood.

Goldberg (1995), in his work *The Problem of Perversion*, extensively discussed how the deficit of this internal idealizing self function is often addressed via the patient's "sexualization of the deficit." Rachel's self doubt and ambivalence about her being lesbian or heterosexual is much more about her feeling anchored and safe rather than being confused about her sexual identity per se; the sexual confusion problem actually puts a "patch" over her deeper fragmentation anxieties. The crises arise when the patch is ripped off.

Dr. Steinman notes:
"There were a number of crises, several additional sessions, and times that the parents had to go on an all night watch to ensure their daughter's safety. But the trend was toward Rachel understanding her thoughts and behavior."

The general rule about psychotic patients is that when they come off antipsychotics they will regress and become psychotic again. Usually this is stated as a categorical imperative for maintaining people who have been psychotic on antipsychotics for life. Of course people are likely to become psychotic again; the trick is to interpretively explore the conflict-laden material, understanding full well that regression to a psychotic, delusional mode of functioning is likely to occur. What is necessary for the therapist is an orientation that delusions and hallucinations, like fantasies, dreams and imagery, can be interpretively explored and resolved.

Gradually, over a period of several months, Rachel timidly worked through rage at her father, finally yelling at him without decompensating after he made a remark that seemed inconsequential to everyone else. She carried on about his organizing the world around himself and dealing with others in a guilt-inducing fashion in order to get his way. She carried on until she understood both the dynamics of her response and the extremity of her outburst.

Here too, there were a number of nights when Rachel would call frantically, saying that the voice was telling her to hurt herself, or after she had burned or cut herself. All of these phenomena were explored and dealt with interpretively and empathically and seen as her difficulty in dealing with guilt and anger, punishing herself rather than dealing with her anger at her father.

Deepening the treatment

"Over the next ten months of therapy, Rachel became more able to deal with her self mutilation around the issue of anger; the voice became less present as an expression of guilt over anger. Extremely strong guilt and trepidation remained, however, around the issues of sexuality. There were frequent retreats into the voice and suicidal thoughts as we looked at the guilt Rachel felt about her sexuality. Often she would leave the office with the voice chastising her, after having volunteered some sexual thoughts or fantasies. Sometimes she would wander dazed; occasionally there were suicidal commands as an expression of guilt about her being interested in sexual things. At times, she needed a low dose of antipsychotic medication to calm down. In phone calls after these periods, and in later sessions, the upsurge of hallucinations and suicidality was seen as a retreat from Rachel's own conflicts about sexuality and an attempt on her part to put the intrapsychic conflict outside herself in the form of the voice. Instead of a person with conflicting impulses and inhibitions, Rachel saw herself as being pursued by deprecating

> voices coming from outside of herself; developing self worth was the operative goal."

Here was the deficit under the sexuality band aid.

This type of material persisted for several more months, with Rachel taking two steps forward and one and a half steps backward. She gradually became more intact, enough so that she could travel with a friend for a month. She then returned to therapy for her last few months before returning to the school she had dropped out of three years before.

At this point, a very interesting episode occurred in Rachel's treatment with Dr. Steinman:

> "Rachel came to a session ashen and tremulous. Slowly and tentatively, amid disclaimers, she told me what happened. She had gone out dancing and couldn't take her eyes off the men's genitals. It upset her terribly that she could be interested in sexuality, especially men's sexuality."

There followed several more retreats into hallucinations berating Rachel for her "disgusting" nature, followed by suicidal ideation. These were explored and understood as her desire to evade dealing with those aspects of herself that were interested in sexuality. Her all or nothing views protected her from the shades of gray and conflicting impulses that make up a more mature intrapsychic life.

The fear of retraumatization

Rachel's work with Dr. Steinman rekindled a developmentally arrested self struggling to find a foothold in self confidence. Borrowing and building on the safety she felt with him and building a more durable safety by finding that she could regroup after falling back into hallucinations and suicidal feelings. Rachel's self was strengthening. It is significant to note that the frequent (but more plastic) retreats into psychosis that Rachel evidenced might best be viewed as "fears of retraumatization" rather than as her evoking psychotic defense mechanisms. What is the trauma that Rachel eschews? We notice above in her reference to her dad that she felt that his anger, his controlling nature and, perhaps most importantly, her inability to find in him an understanding of herself, led her to fear Dr. Steinman's own responses to her swirling currents of self doubt and confusion. Her own anger and guilty feelings were unbearable until they could be held and tolerated in the therapy. Steinman's steadfast attitude that these unbearable affects could be tolerated and understood formed the basis for the cycles of disruption and repair that are signals as to the development of a strengthening self.

Affect bearing and desexualization of the deficit

"There followed a number of terrified and disorganized episodes, which Rachel was able to see as her reluctance to accept an emerging interest in sexuality. As we talked, she began to tell me about the rules and strictures against sexuality in her family.

As far as Rachel was concerned, her mother's attitude toward sexuality was only negative. I told Rachel that this was an intrapsychic problem; should her mother come in with her and reassure her that sex was all right, she would still feel guilty about her sexuality until she worked through her own conflicts.

The very next session, Rachel brought her mother in with her, thinking I had suggested that her mother come in. After I pointed out Rachel's ambivalence about ameliorating her harsh, internal attitude toward sex, essentially bringing in her mother on her own volition, the three of us discussed Rachel and sexuality.

We had a very useful and clarifying talk. First, Rachel had accurately registered and then adopted some of her mother's tenets about sensual life. Secondly, the mother said that at the time she gave birth to Rachel's younger sisterr, she had quickly toilet trained Rachel (some sixteen months old) with some stern injunctions and comments about 'that dirty area'.

Thirdy, Rachel's mother thought she was going to be pregnant, with Rachel, before her wedding day.

This information, although somewhat difficult for Rachel's mother to present, aided Rachel greatly in modifying her own harshly critical attitudes toward sex. Rachel realized that her own mother's conscious values about sex were markedly different from what Rachel had fantasized these values to be."

Note the presence of exploration, curiosity and comfort with the body self.

Rachel became quite forthcoming in her discussion of her sexuality, bringing up dreams and fantasies and recollections about being interested in sexuality. She became able to masturbate without guilt, stopped retreating into hallucinations, and became quite interested in talking about many aspects of sex.

Leaving psychosis behind

"During this period of psychotherapy, Rachel was no longer psychotic. She had no delusions, no voices and no regressions to terrified self states and suicidal thoughts. Hallucinations, self-mutilating behaviour, regressive retreats, and the upsurge of psychotic thinking had been understood as a retreat from intrapsychic conflict. They did not return during the remainder of treatment with me."

Dr. Steinman continues:

"After several more months, Rachel returned to the university in the Midwest with the recommendation that she stay in psychodynamically oriented psychotherapy. Perhaps there were more layers of the onion to be peeled. Before leaving for school she presented me with a poem celebrating her sexuality, a first for her, since so much of her other writing over the previous years had celebrated death.

Three years later she graduated with honours and dedicated her thesis to me. That dedication told me that the gains of therapy were still holding then. The gains have continued over the intervening years. Significantly, Rachel remembers the most important lesson: we were able to deal with psychotic and suicidal behaviour through an in-depth psychodynamic understanding; such knowledge, wherever it leads, will stand her in good stead. Thirty years later, when I tracked Rachel down to get her permission to publish this material, she told me several important things.

Firstly, in a later psychotherapy with a woman, she uncovered memories of sexual trauma by her father. She said that it would have been too hard to discuss this kind of material with an older male psychiatrist, even if she had remembered it at the time of our work together. As several of the other cases in this book make clear, physical or sexual abuse can readily lead to the development of psychosis. I only wish that Rachel and I could have sorted out this material in our work together, but it sometimes takes a prolonged time to uncover and deal with such painful material.

Secondly, and most importantly for the purposes of this book, Rachel told me that since our work together she had had no hallucinations or voice telling her what to do. This young, allegedly schizophrenic woman took the insights of our therapy together and maintained her gains and sanity over the intervening thirty years, even uncovering painful details of trauma, without retreating into psychosis or needing antipsychotic medication.

Gracious and generous as usual, Rachel penned the following note: "You also have my deep appreciation for your efforts to change the assumption that people who need antipsychotic medication at one point will need to take that medication for the rest of their lives. I have benefited profoundly from your progressive perspectives about the role of medication in supporting therapy, not replacing it." Such a result is not only a testament to Rachel's intelligence and desire to understand herself but a further example of the transforming power and life-saving effectiveness of intensive psychotherapy in those once so disturbed."

CHAPTER SIX

Three rats and the extraterrestrial

Lois was a depressed, withdrawn, woman in her mid thirties, when she consulted Dr. Steinman. She had a previous diagnosis of chronic paranoid schizophrenia, had been hospitalized several times and had been treated for the previous seven years with antipsychotics. She had lived in a half-way house for the better part of a year and now lived alone in a rooming house. She was unkempt, disheveled, clearly preoccupied, and hallucinating.

She had been married, but was now divorced. She had given up custody of her children, and had had a persistent delusion for years that three rats were gnawing away at her. She had little contact with anyone except for an old friend of hers who sent her to Dr. Steinman. By everyone's account, previous friends, family, psychiatrists, and ancillary staff, she was a burnt out case.

The diagnosis of chronic schizophrenia had been made during one of her first hospitalizations, when she told a psychiatrist about the three rats gnawing at her.

Living without a net

People with delusions are beset by beliefs, images and a concatenation of feelings that it is impossible for them to bear, at least to bear in their current vulnerable state. Hence the delusion, the projection outside of themselves of issues they can't handle. Like Freud's notion of the return of the repressed, having to do with issues one has put out of consciousness coming back to bedevil one, these people—perhaps due to a greater imaginative quality, perhaps a poorer synthetic ability, perhaps more pain and trauma in life—project issues outside of themselves.

Self psychology sees delusions from a slightly different vantage. All of the above reflections remain, but what the psychology of the self adds in is that a delusional system is a compensatory structure that prevents fragmentation.

Projected issues however, are like a tethered rubber ball on a paddle, they keep coming back to where they began. The fearful, isolated, lonely, paranoid patient gets the interest and involvement he craves, but without a selfobject experience the anxiety, fears and, at times, terror never abates. In the delusion may lie a key to the code of the person's thinking. Sometimes, as our previous cases illustrate, it may take years to establish a durable enough selfobject experience to be able to escort the patient into a more secure internal mileu; here in this case it was much simpler.

Dr. Steinman quickly saw that the opening lay in the rats gnawing at her. A self psychologically oriented psychoanalyst will want to understand this from the most "experience-near" perspective possible. Did they mean anything to her? Not surprisingly, she hadn't been asked that question by previous psychiatrists or even thought very much about the meaning of such a powerful image. In some regards, it is strange that a person can be totally immersed in a terrifying or otherwise very upsetting series of thoughts or a delusion, and not think at all as to why they're having such thoughts. How can patient or psychiatrist make sense of bizarre delusions if they never discuss their possible content, meaning and the affect contained within? As we have seen before, without enough "psychological oxygen" (Kohut, 1971) provided by a selfobject experience, the patient is left at the whim and fury of all sorts of terrifying perceptual experiences.

Dr. Steinman ponders:

"What did the three rats mean? She didn't know. I had some sense immediately, for she had three children. When did the image begin? Lois noted that it was during the long (six month) hospitalization after the birth of her youngest child, when she couldn't bear to see them, felt terribly guilty about being away from them, yet she felt completely unable to handle any interaction with them. Could the number 'three' relate to her three children I asked, burrowing into her as her own feelings of loss and guilt about not being involved with her three children burrowed into her? She hadn't thought about such a possibility."

This not having thought about it is a part of the difficulty in a delusional person. Such a person needs help to understand the meaning of his productions, the psychological mechanisms involved and, most of all, to deal with the underlying feelings that led to the formation of delusions. This is why it is essential that the treating psychiatrist or therapist attempt to help clarify the ramifications of delusions and hallucinations. To not do so, to diagnose and medicate alone, often leaves a patient without a channel to understanding themselves. Yet, explanations are not curative. As mentioned earlier, we view symptoms as breakdown products of a previously intact self.

In order for a strengthening and rebalancing to take hold, the patient must experience an empathic connection between themselves and the clinician.

The nature of delusion in self psychology

Not all delusions are persecutory. In mania and in depression, one can find delusional phenomena at work. Some delusions operate on a continuum from "over valued ideas" to frank delusions and exhibit a certain fluidity whereas others are quite fixed, rigid, and unrelenting. Let's listen back to the great phenomenologist Karl Jaspers:

> We can then distinguish two large groups of delusion according to their "origin": one group "emerges understandably" from preceding affects, from shattering, mortifying, guilt-provoking or other such experiences, from false-perceptions or from the experience of de realization in states of altered consciousness, etc. The other

group is for us "psychologically irreducible"; phenomenologically it is something final. We give the term "delusion-like ideas" to the first group; the latter we term "delusions proper." In their case we must now try and get closer to the facts of the delusional experience itself ... (Jaspers, 1963, p. 96)

Jaspers goes on to look at three distinct possibilities:

"the first step is an *awareness of change in one's personality*, much as one might feel, for instance, if one had put on a uniform for the first time and felt conspicuous. So paranoiacs think that the change in themselves, which they alone appreciate is also noticed by their environment.

From this delusion that *one has become noticeable* arises the delusion that one is watched and from that, the delusion that one is being persecuted ... the same may be said for the attempt to derive delusion from preceding affects, the affect of distrust, for instance ... we are only offered an understandable context for the emergence of certain stubborn misconceptions ... we find every degree of mental defect without delusions of any kind and the most fantastic and incredible delusions in the case of people of superior intelligence. The critical faculty is not obliterated but "put into the service of the delusion." ... We have to assume some "specific alteration in psychic function ... delusion ... as a psychological product, it is a 'mental creation' ... from the point of view of meaningful connections, it is motivated, dynamic content." (Jaspers, 1963, pp. 96–98. Italics added for emphasis)

Deficit states that occur as a result of trauma or the combination of vulnerability and trauma can lead to severe disruptions in the structure of the self. Although there is a risk in reification, we can begin to think of what Jasper (1963) calls "primary delusion" as an endogenous, internally erected scaffolding and we might define it as a "self state structure" or a "compensatory structure."

Think back to Kohut's discussion of the Schreber case in the lectures he gave to the candidates at the Chicago Institute where he moves away from the issue of unconscious homosexuality being the cause of paranoid delusions to his image of the patient finding himself on unstable, precarious ground at the edge of a cliff, desperately hanging on to the edge (Tolpin & Tolpin, 1996, pp. 282–283). Recall also, page nine of "Introductory Considerations" in Kohut's 1971 volume on *The Analysis of the Self*, wherein he diagrams the breakdown of the idealizing selfobject—"Development and regression in the realm of the omnipotent object." Here "Nuclei (fragments) of the idealized omnipotent object; disjointed mystical religious feeling; vague awe" (Kohut, 1971, p. 9) are the descriptors Kohut attributes to the experience of an insidious de-idealization.

Garfield and Havens (1991, 1993) pointed out that in paranoia and pathological narcissism, a breakdown in idealized experience and the experience of "having the rug pulled out from under you" leaves the patient in a self state where there is an imminent threat of "falling" into a total collapse. Delusion thus serves as a "self state remedy" or a "delusionalization of the deficit" that protects the patient from implosion.

Delusion as defensive compensatory structure

Let's return to Dr. Steinman and Lois:

> "She agreed that the rats might represent her three children gnawing at her feelings. She seemed comforted by this sense, and much more willing to bring up historical and, gradually, emotional material that had persisted for many years."

Lois was an only child of a critical and negative mother and a loving, indulgent father. Her father loved her unconditionally and served as a buffer against the constant jibes and denigrating comments of her mother. Her mother excoriated her; her father extolled her. When she was seven, she and her father were told by her intimidating, extremely impressive old Russian ballet teacher that she "dances like she comes from another planet."

Later, this comment by her ballet teacher evolved into a fantasy and then served as the seed of a delusion, a delusion from those early years of life that she came from outer space. If she did come from outer space, this might account for her mother's criticism and caustic comments. She was sheltered in her father's love, because he too must come from outer space; her mother must be an earthling, jealous of her extraterrestrial origin. Such a belief comforted her and seemed innocuous, but it was laden with unforeseen difficulty.

Forces of traumatic de-idealization

When she was thirteen, her father died unexpectedly. In a normal idealizing channel, small, digestible disruptions in the idealizing experience result in normal self-strengthening development via the process Kohut (1971) described as "transmuting internalization." Here, children are able, over time, to internalize the self-esteem, self-regulating functions previously provided by the ideal. Larger or deeper disappointments or losses can lead to a "traumatic de-idealization" resulting in developmental arrest or worse. When your "safety net" is ripped away from you, some solution to the anxiety of falling off a cliff must be found.

Lois was grief-stricken and had to be hospitalized for a number of months. During those months she did the expected, the expected for someone who has broken the bounds of reality. She created another delusion, this time of "her father always with her."

> Dr. Steinman notes:
> "She had never talked of this belief to anyone before, neither when hospitalized in her early teens nor during later hospitalizations and other periods of psychotherapy. She felt safe enough to tell me this, perhaps because she had been so frightened of the three rats which we had deciphered, perhaps because she felt we both could speak the same language, the language of understanding; we could converse about the meaning of delusional imagery."

Since his death more than twenty years ago, her father had been by her side all her waking life. When she passed someone a cup of coffee, she passed him one too. When she went bicycling, he went along on his own bike. Whatever she did, she was accompanied by her much loved father. He was kept healthy and whole in her delusional reality; as far as Lois was concerned, her father remained vibrant and alive, not moldering and decaying in the ground. Long days and nights, when she was apparently alone, were spent immersed in conversation and delight with her lost and protective father.

Some kind of footing is better than none

Lois kept her delusion a secret, probably because some part of her knew her father was dead and she didn't want to disrupt her internal world with the harsh world of a reality that included her continuously sniping and now depressed mother and the fact that her father had died. She appeared to the world to have recovered from the serious decompensation that had led to her adolescent hospitalization, but internally she maintained a rich and vivid delusional life through her ongoing activities with her father.

Externally, Lois appeared to keep it together, enough so that she married in her late teens. Yet internal preoccupations make choosing a stable spouse difficult. In her early twenties, she went further into her comforting delusions of her father when her first husband committed suicide by hanging, for no apparent reason other than that he was doing drugs at the time. With the internal fabric of psyche ripped away from her again, this sudden, unexpected and additional loss reinforced her retreat into a delusional world with her father. Several years later she married a very understanding, solid man who looked after her until she decompensated after the birth of their third child.

The problem with delusion as compensatory structure

In the *Restoration of the Self* (1977), Kohut elucidated how deficits in self structure result in psychopathology. He differentiated between compensatory structure which provides a connection between the patient and either mirroring, idealizing, or twinship "poles" of the self *vs.* defensive or deficient compensatory structures. He remarks,

> I call a structure defensive when its sole or predominant function is the covering over of the primary defect in the self. I call a structure compensatory when, it compensates for this defect. Undergoing a development of its own, it brings about a functional rehabilitation of the self by making up for the weakness in one pole of the self through the strengthening of the other pole. Most frequently a weakness in the area of exhibitionism and ambitions (*mirroring*), is compensated for by the self-esteem provided by the pursuit of ideals (*idealizing*); but the reverse may also occur. (Kohut, 1977, pp. 3–4; italics added)

With respect to Lois, her quiet delusion expanded quickly after the death of an important man and then, later, with the birth of a child which may have "overextended" the parent/child need she already felt was so lacking. It comes as no surprise that she turned inward to the fantasied/delusional structure of her father with more commitment. With the continual tearing away at the earlier self structure, Lois's preoccupation with her self created relationship with her father served almost as a "vascular" stent that allowed her to keep her affective lifeblood flowing.

A delusional reality is both fragile and rigid. Patients cling to delusions. Lois had had two very important losses which she attempted to deal with by creating the delusional reality of her comforting father. Now, with the breakdown after her third child in her thirties, she developed persecutory delusions that terrified her, in addition to the delusion of the rats gnawing away at her heart.

Once delusional, one is always vulnerable to delusional crises and regressions, until the delusions and the mechanisms of delusion formation are explored, understood, and sustainable in a human way that connects to authentic sources of self-regard. This requires the establishment of an idealizing selfobject experience that allows for reconstruction. Once one has fractured the bounds of reality, for whatever reason, one is prone to increasing delusion formation to offset potential new unbalanced threats to the self.

What harm is there in the protective delusion of the father to help an adolescent cope with his death? The harm lies in the unrepaired rend in the fabric of the psyche and thus, increasing propensity to develop all types of delusions, running the gamut from protective to playful to destructive and terrorizing as a way of dealing with unbearable anxiety. In the process, one's actual self gets buried under a layer of self obfuscating phenomena. Kohut discusses how a healthy self evolves:

> When, 1) after the analytic penetration of the defensive structures, the primary defect in the self has been exposed and via working through and transmuting internalization, sufficiently filled out so that the formerly defective structures of the self have now become functionally reliable 2) .... after the patient has achieved cognitive and affective mastery with regard to the defenses surrounding the primary defect in the self, with regard to the compensatory structures and with regard to the relationship between these—the compensatory structures have now become functionally reliable, independent of the area in which this success was achieved.

... through improvements in the area of the primary defect, or through, the analysis of the vicissitudes of the compensatory structures (including the healing of their structural deficiencies ...). (Kohut, 1977, p. 4)

The healing of delusion and defensive compensatory structure

In the telling of her delusions and history, with a little prodding from Dr. Steinman about how difficult it was to accept her father's death, her mother's neglect and abusiveness, and the other pains of life, Lois established an ongoing and durable idealizing selfobject experience with him. She was then able to give up her delusions in the following fashion. She recognized how the belief that she was an extraterrestrial was a way of seeming important and special, as she had seemed special to her ballet teacher and father. It was a way to protect her from her mother, and give importance to her own existence.

The delusion of her father being constantly with her dissipated over a period of about three months, with a few several day hospitalizations to keep her from harming herself. Giving up this delusion was risky. Not only was it comforting, but she had never been able to mourn her father's death twenty years earlier. Here we see improvement of the primary defect with the mourning process of unbearable grief becoming bearable with Dr. Steinman's steadfast attention. This relinquishing of the delusion of her father was aided by the development of a transitional, short term delusion of her three children constantly by her side. In short, she substituted her children for her father as the "delusionalization of the deficit." Rather than being an impediment, though, this new delusion was a flash of inspiration and a therapeutic aid, when Dr. Steinman suggested that the new delusion of her children constantly with her was pointing her toward making contact with her ex husband to see if she could become involved in her childrens' lives.

Dr. Steinman noted:
"We were able to talk about her yearning for those she loved, whether father or estranged children. She used delusions as a way of believing she was in contact with loved ones, all the while feeling

powerless to actually be in contact with loved ones. Delusions were seen as her yearning for those she loved."

With this change of focus toward the world, and an emphasis on the means of reconciling with her children (a definite possibility as opposed to being in touch with her long dead father), Lois was able to shift her attention from her delusional compensations and focused all her energy on her children. Without internal delusions taking up her loving vital energy, she was able to re-establish a very good and ongoing relationship with her children. In addition, she became quite successful at two differing careers, neither of which was ballet.

Dr. Steinman:
"Her twenty year long delusional orientation dissolved over a six to eight month period. We had talked her language in such a way that her psychic energy could travel outward toward life, instead of incessantly cycling inwardly toward blockage and death. She finished therapy, having more than achieved gains for which she had never dared to hope. Over the years, she has kept in touch by mail, having maintained the gains of an exploratory psychotherapy of delusions, without resort to dramatic and delusional compensations for unbearable feeling states Thirty years later, she contacted me after hearing me talking on the radio. The gains of an intensive psychotherapy had continued. She had remarried, was an active grandmother and continued working in her chosen field. She had never had to resort to delusions or hallucinations; she never again needed antipsychotic medication. Her 'chronic paranoid schizophrenia' had never returned. To me, this repreents a talking cure, via intensive psychotherapy, of a previously debilitating case of chronic paranoid schizophrenia."

PART III

ALIKENESS (TWINSHIP)

CHAPTER SEVEN

Jonathan and the twinship transference

Jonathan would have been noticeable in any crowd. His full red beard swept below his knees; his unkempt, knotted hair reached his ankles, snaking through curious tortured curls, as it drooped toward the ground. His eyes were glazed and other-worldly, as he sat in Dr. Steinman's waiting room.

Jonathan had been psychotic for nearly twenty-five years, and had not benefited from the various psychiatrists and antipsychotic medicines he had taken over that time. Thus, his family figured they had nothing to lose by dragging him in to see the new psychiatrist they had heard about though a friend.

Dragging him in is what they had to do, for Jonathan's mind was elsewhere. His gaunt, spare frame and seer visage belied an inner preoccupation with something unseen by the rest of us. When his elder brother tried to get Jonathan to come in to the office, Jonathan barely moved. Slowly, with much urging and pulling from his brother and exhortations from his mother, he stood up. After five minutes, he haltingly walked, slow, hesitating step by slow hesitating step, through the doorway; in another five minutes, he had moved about eight feet.

His brother pulled, but Jonathan became more difficult to move. He was mute and began to show the waxy flexibility, psychiatrists associate with catatonia. Catatonia is relatively rare these days, either because patients are usually medicated or our social milieu has changed. Generally speaking, catatonia was presumed to be a state in which patients did not communicate.

Psychoanalysts, long ago, came to the conclusion that even "non-communicative" patients were communicating something, whether it was anger, an inner preoccupation, avoidance of contact or involvement with hallucinations and delusional figures.

Dr. Steinman begins:
"What's making it so hard to come in the office?"
Silence; the glazed look persisted.
Dr. Steinman had seen this before and assumed Jonathan was otherwise preoccupied. "Your attention appears to be somewhere else. Coming into the office or not doesn't appear to be very high on your list of priorities."
He hovered several feet inside the office. His family came in with him, closed the door and sat down.
"Tea, anyone?"
They demurred. Dr. Steinman poured himself a cup of jasmine tea and sat down.
Jonathan still hung there, a thin, bird like presence.
"What's going on Jonathan?"
Again, nothing.
Over the next half an hour, Jonathan stood, as Dr. Steinman tried to get him to talk. He wouldn't respond to direct questions about why it was so hard to sit down, or what preoccupied him. He would move forward a step or two into the office, then back to where he started. His eyes had a far-away look.
"You look really undecided about coming in to my office, Jonathan. You move forward, then backwards and you seem focused on something else, something other than here."
Again, silence.
The psychiatrist turned to the family. "How long has Jonathan been like this?"
His brother Dan replied.

"Months; he blew up at his girlfriend's and threw a computer. He has been living with us ever since. He hardly eats or drinks and stays by himself in his room."

"And his hair and beard! They're so long," chimed in his elderly mother. "I want him to cut them, but he won't."

With catatonic schizophrenia staring them in the face, his mother wanted him to get a shave and a haircut; "shades of the sixties" Dr. Steinman thought.

"Jonathan. Are you listening to something? Is something telling you what to do?"

"Barber," he blurted out.

"Barber?" "What does 'barber' mean?"

Jonathan said nothing, but in a slow, methodical, otherworldly way, sat down. That was all he said for the rest of the session, as he stared into the distance, nodding and shaking his head and muttering unintelligible words to himself.

"What are you saying?"

Again, nothing.

"You seem to be saying lots of different things. Are you hearing different things? Are you thinking different things?"

Private and undecipherable words ensued, along with some more nodding and shaking of his head in response to internal stimuli. For all practical purposes he had communicated as much as we could piece together that first session.

The family said they could handle him at home. I asked Jonathan if he would take any medicine; he remained mute. The family doubted if he would take anything; he had tried a number of antipsychotics over the previous twenty-five years, with no beneficial effects.

As Dr. Steinman tossed around various alternatives as to what to do with this very fragile man, it seemed that the best course would be to have his family look after him; they seemed willing and caring. He seemed far too disturbed to be put into the hospital, where he might easily deteriorate and would have to be forcibly medicated. In addition, his family provided food, shelter, and housing so he could not be put into the hospital against his will.

"Good to meet you all; let's talk again tomorrow. Call me if you are having trouble with Jonathan. Here's a night-time number, if you need it."

Dan gently pulled Jonathan out of his chair and the three of them, ever so slowly, left for the day.

As they left, Steinman wondered. "Had I done the right thing? Should I have tried to hospitalize him against his will, even though this might not have succeeded? Should I have insisted that he take antipsychotic medicines? He didn't think so, but what would happen if Jonathan decompensated further at home that evening? Perhaps, in time, he would take some meds; maybe they would even help this time."

Had anything been accomplished? Most importantly, Jonathan was treated in a way that regarded him as a person and he had not been coerced.

First impressions: vitality affects revisited

Imagine you are seeing what Dr. Steinman sees. The first thing you notice about Jonathan is "His full red beard swept below his knees; his unkempt, knotted hair reaching his ankles, 'snaking' through tortured curls, as it droops toward the ground."

Our temptation is to interpret this amazingly rich visual depiction. But let us rather stay with our own infrastructure of our own visual system. Our eyes take a downward, slow, spiral course from head to toe.

Heinz Werner (1948), the famous comparative developmental psychologist at Clark University in Worcester Massachusetts in the US, coined the unwieldy term "physiognomic perception." In 1932, he noted that objects are first perceived by their dynamic inner tensions rather than by the objective technical features. Werner also emphasized that objects can be perceived in one sensory domain and automatically translated to another sensory mode—he called this "sensorium commune."

Moving forward, sixty years to many infant researchers like Tronick (1978), Meltzoff (1979), and Gropnik (1988), and the well known psychoanalyst and developmental infant researcher, Dan Stern. Upending some of Piaget's (1959) most cherished concepts of how perception occurs, these researchers also discovered, as did Werner, that humans have something called "cross modal perception." What does that mean? That means that the rhythm, frequency, intensity, and duration experienced in one sensory mode automatically is understood in all sensory modes. A strobe light flashing at a certain frequency and at a certain lumen intensity in our visual field, will, in the infrastructure of our minds, match up exactly with a sound that has a certain beat, decibel level and duration. Not only that, but it generates, on the keyboard of our soul, an identical mood and feeling state.

Dan Stern's 2004 and 2010 books, *The Present Moment in Psychotherapy and Everyday Life* and *Forms of Vitality* explore the modern iteration of Werner's "physiognomic perception" and cultivates those seeds as they germinate into a garden of what he calls "vitality affects." These are forms of feelings, grounded in the body's movement. Here is where motion meets emotion. Breathing, swallowing, urinating and even falling asleep can all carry, on their back, moods and feelings. We jump in surprise. We also "rise up" in anger. We collapse in grief. We dance with joy. We hold our breath with anticipatory hope and fear. We sigh with relief. We are an orchestrated affective canon, sonata, opera, and haiku.

The present moment lasts from four to ten seconds Stern tells us. It takes three or four to trace Jonathan's beard down to his toes if we seriously take it all in. Stern notes that the artist paints a picture that we think is static and stationary and yet, there is always movement depicted in it. Our eyes are guided by brush strokes in this way and that. All of this generates a set of feelings and creates a host of moods that wash over the viewer.

This is true of Jonathan. He is one very "slowed down" guy according to the visual of his beard. His psychiatric psychotic melancholia is tortuous, we are told, as his beard cascades slowly in a spiral fashion downward. He barely moves. His family is heartbroken. They can hardly move him. Indeed, he is catatonic.

The next day

Gaunt and ethereal, Jonathan came in again with his family. His face turned from side to side as he muttered to himself.

>"What's that?" Dr. Steinman asked about the muttering.
>"Rob, Bob."
>"Who's Rob? Who's Bob?"
>Without missing a beat, Jonathan starts in.
>"Bob is my father; he has always been a part of my life. Bob is floating around in time. He died a few months ago. Rob is the

opposite, someone else who came along, after Bob died, Bob without the R."

Werner's collaborator, Bernard Kaplan (1984) noted that most developmental-stage frameworks focus on structures that undergo progressive differentiation (Piaget, 1952) A. Freud, 1966; Vaillant, (1977). Kaplan's view was primarily functional and he emphasized the progressive elaboration and hierarchic integration of language usage. Thus, the function that language in communication subserves is the central question for Kaplan. Kaplan borrowed from Ombredance (1951) the five stages of affective, ludic, pragmatic, representational, and dialectical language function. "Affective" usage is illustrated in how people use prosody, pitch, variation, tone, and word/sentence choice to convey mood. The second stage that Kaplan described is that of "ludic" usage where the interaction and its linguistic medium serve the function of play.

Garvey (1977) looked at how children play with noises and sounds. "Syllable shapes and prosodic features such as intonation and stress provide the raw material for early language play. Controlled variation in articulation, such as rasping, whispering or nasalization, are also favorite materials" (Garvey, 1977, p. 61). In adult communication, the ludic function is present but, for the most part, goes unmarked. Is Jonathan playing with Dr. Steinman in his word salad? Is this, as Winnicott might call it, the beginning of a "chumship"?

"Were you close to your father?"

"Very close. We used to hike a lot and he'd talk about everything."

"Did you talk too?"

"Not much."

"Why are you saying Rob, Bob?"

"They're saying it. I'm just repeating what they're telling me."

"Who's saying it?"

"People."

"Like who?"

"Bill, Bill Bradley. JFK. People are there."

"People?"

"Representations, voices of people. Someone said he told me that, Bill Bradley, because he didn't want someone else, JFK. There are criminals and crooks saying I didn't offer due respect. He's gay. Queer or straight."

"How many representations or presences or voices are there?" Here Dr. Steinman wants to get a feeling for what the person is dealing with; seeing how long it took him to get into the office yesterday, the sense was that there were a very large number of voices.

"A lot, so many."

"How long have they been there?"

Jonathan pauses, looks pensive and responds breathily.

"Early in my life, I was whole. I was myself until 1979, twenty-five years ago. Then I had a dream. A fist went through a glass shower door. When I woke up, I felt the balance of my life had changed. My unity was shattered. Then they started talking to me. Much of my time is spent observing these people talking, or my physiology."

Selfobject functions

The purpose of selfobjects or selfobject experiences (Stolorow & Lachmann, 1980) in psychosis is to reverse the tide of fragmentation, loss of positive affective coloring and loss of the continuity of time. Schizophrenia used to be known for massive distortion of temporality as patients became "prisoners of the present." Not only was this an allusion to Freud's idea that the unconscious erupts into the conscious, but, as there is no time in the unconscious, there can only be the unending experience of being trapped in the present. The future is elusive and the past is detached and lost. Jonathan on the other hand, has a reasonable mood at this time and is grounded in time. Yet, we have massive fragmentation at our doorstep. This is a man in need of anti-fragmentation. The clinical question is whether Jonathan can make use of Dr. Steinman in this way.

As an interesting aside, Jonathan's fragmentation sits in juxtaposition to another presentation of psychosis: the delusion. An "authochthonus" delusion is one that appears immediately and in full form. It is "made manifest." It is almost indestructible in the way it instantly congeals. As mentioned before, the delusion is compensatory structure that connects mental content. It condenses mental contents rather than dispersing them.

Dr. Steinman continues:

"To you they're people?"

"Of course."

"And they've been there for how long?"

"About twenty-five years." Jonathan spoke in a thin, reedy voice with barely enough force in it to be heard.

"Do you talk much with these people?"

"No; I just listen."

"Who else is there besides JFK and Bill Bradley?"

"Stu, my cousin."

"Anyone else?"

"Lots."

"For example?"

"Bad people. Good people. Principled people. Working people. Philosophers. Stupid people." This last comment he spat out.

"Why do you say stupid people like that?"

"I didn't say it; they did."

Jonathan had begun to talk, responding to questions and observations. Perhaps sitting and talking was similar to his father and he walking and his father talking. They left, Jonathan again pulled by his brother Dan.

As they left, Jonathan's mother chimed in, "He hasn't talked this much in years and years."

What had happened here? How had someone who looked like a regressed, catatonic schizophrenic on one day—and had for a more than twenty years previously—suddenly been able to start to articulate what was going on within him? Several possibilities come to mind. Perhaps he had transferred positive feelings from his father onto Dr. Steinman.

Another possibility was that he was speaking about his internal world, and we were trying to make sense of it. The psychiatrist conveyed to him and his family that they were on a journey of exploration, trying to make sense of Jonathan and how he thought and why he thought as he did. With judgment and criticism left at the door, many patients begin to feel free to engage.

Interestingly, Dr. Steinman was pretty conversant with Jonathan's spiritual and philosophical interests as well.

A spiritual seeker

Jonathan was a mystic, a spiritual seeker after truth through meditation and contemplation. He had lived for the last thirty-five years the life of a seer. Though it was easy to view him as a chronic schizophrenic, he was also the genuine article, a "baba lover," a lover of his notions of god, and a man who pursued the blissful states of consciousness elaborated in Hindu thought. It was as if Sri Aurabindo's "The Life Divine" had become manifest in Jonathan.

Dr. Steinman knew something about this, having dabbled in spirituality in the sixties, like many of the generation, reading and meditating on Vedic, Hindu, Taoist, and Buddhist religious and philosophical texts. His office has artifacts from a number of different religions and cultures, Egyptian, Buddhist, Afghan, Polynesian, Japanese, African, Iranian, Hindu, and Chinese. Perhaps Jonathan felt at home in the seeming office chaos of so many images and so many world views that were important and familiar to him.

Developmental history

Jonathan had grown up in a small community, the youngest son; his seven year older brother was always very helpful and caring. His mother controlling and loving, his father a professional man who was a good provider, but somewhat removed emotionally. The family moved to San Francisco early in grammar school.

Jonathan did very well in school, had numerous friends and accomplished a lot. He played sports, was on teams, became an Eagle Scout and the leader of his chapter of Boy Scouts. When he went off to college, he thought he'd pursue a professional career.

In college, he felt a little unhinged. He was interested in girls, but no one serious. He smoked some grass and drank for the first eight months, then stopped all substances, wanting to get his life together. He did fine scholastically and socially, but was a little nervous at school, so began practicing a variety of meditation that was then current. He fell in love with a girl who also practiced meditation and the two of them went off to Israel for a semester, where they both worked on a kibbutz. He loved the involvement with the kibbutz and meditation. Though the relationship didn't work out with the girl, he continued practicing meditation and then he returned to college to graduate, having studied both sciences and foreign languages.

He was unsure as to what to do when he finished college. Should he go to graduate school? He liked the meditation that he practiced; it was now 1971. Several of his friends were also practicing the same form of meditation. Little by little he became involved in a religious movement, a cult that practiced this particular form of meditation. Quickly, since he was so smart, ambitious and capable, he worked his way up the hierarchical ladder of his spiritual order. Within several years, he was traveling around the world for this group, both participating in it and teaching its principles. He was pleased by both his pursuits and accomplishments. For ten years, he practiced his meditation, taught and worked as a productive member of the group's hierarchy. He had friends, romances, and involvements.

Then a strange thing happened. He was thirty-two years old. After more than ten years of meditation and spiritual pursuits, Jonathan noticed that the sky became very dark one day, electric feelings began to course through his body. He became frightened, but curious as to what was going on. Suddenly an intense flash of white light rose up in his body and shot out through the front of his chest. Jonathan shot outside of himself to the heavens. After this intense experience, the skies darkened and shifted, swirling around him; he felt frightened and lost.

Separation and fragmentation

Shortly afterward, the voices began. He became increasingly disturbed. The group suggested that he just work in the fields, but he pursued his meditation and inward spiritual quest. After six months or so, when he didn't improve, they suggested that he leave the administrative center of the group. They sent him to psychiatrists, but Jonathan would always stop the antipsychotics he was started on. At first he tried drugs like Haldol and Stelazine. More recently, he had tried Risperdal, Seroquel, and Zyprexa, but always quickly stopped them, complaining of side effects.

He lived with his family for a while, maintaining a peripheral involvement with his group; whenever he went to training sessions or retreats, he would be sent home because he acted so strangely. Where the group wanted a little meditation once, perhaps twice a day, Jonathan—always the Eagle Scout—pursued his internal preoccupations and meditations for many hours a day. His group used meditation as a guide to a practical life; Jonathan used it as a means of union with the god-head.

Reaching out and not connecting: the forward edge

In the process he got lost. He became involved with a woman in the group. She was extremely disturbed in her own right, but the two carved out a life together in which they would meditate and go into their own internal worlds, for the most part living lives in parallel, he in his and she in hers.

The family helped out a bit with his finances while he lived in San Francisco.

In the mid nineties, her mother became ill. Jonathan and she moved in to help his girlfriend's invalid mother in another community. His family lost touch with him, as Jonathan and the girlfriend retreated into their own solipsistic reveries in an increasingly cluttered and disheveled household after her mother died. His girlfriend did all the cooking, they would shop together late at night; neither did any cleaning.

Most of his days were spent in what he called meditation. In reality, as gradually became clear, he was either in a state of what he called "spiritual bliss" or preoccupied with one or more of the hundreds of voices to which he listened. He would appear to be sleeping, but really was watching and observing and immersed in the contents of his mind.

On several occasions, Jonathan would be taken to see various psychiatrists as a result of his gesturing, muttering to himself, lack of attention to hygiene and his incessant preoccupation with internal stimuli. Each time he would take some medicine for a few days, then, turn inward, again.

More recently, he had burst out in a fit of anger at the reclusive girlfriend. He had become too terrifying for her to look after. He threw a computer at the wall. The girlfriend called his family who brought him to live with them. He had been with them for about a month. He barely ate or slept. He nodded, muttered, and gesticulated wildly or remained mute and internally focused. At times, he would blurt things out; most of the time he was silent.

The twinship alternative

Jonathan's female companionship can be viewed as an attempt of his to "reach out." He was attempting to be close to someone who he felt shared the same world as he. As noted earlier in this volume, Marian Tolpin (2002) described the "forward edge of transference" as one where one finds vital psychological nutrients. These vitalizing, cohering, and connecting experiences corresponded to Kohut's three types of selfobject transferences: mirroring, idealizing, and twinship transferences. They stand in contrast to the traditional "trailing edge transferences," well known to psychoanalysis as the essential feature of the repetition compulsion. In self psychology, when positive self enhancing experiences are lost, the trailing edge takes over. That is when Jonathan gets lost.

Early on, Kohut (1971) felt that the "alter ego" or "twinship transference" was a form of the mirror transference and that the grandiose self had, within the mirroring transference, developed some degree of separateness from the object. It wasn't until 1984, in *How does Analysis Cure*, that Kohut began to consider the "alter ego" or twinship transference to be another whole category of transference separate from the mirror or idealizing types. He refined this understanding first, in terms of a transference "sui generis" that pertained to one of three areas of selfobject need in normality. The mirroring need for affirmation and recognition at one pole, the idealizing need to merge with calmness and strength at the other pole and, in the intermediate area of talents and skills, a need for an experience with "essential likeness" or deep similarity were outlined. Furthermore, it was in a case of a woman with terrible loneliness, whom Kohut (p. 195) first thought was needing "mirroring experiences" and only later, realized that she was attempting to draw psychological sustenance via an "alter ego" experience. Here she would compulsively and continuously "cover" various home items such as jars or containers. Echoing back to her extremely lonely childhood, she revealed that she would imagine having a genie in a little bottle that she would carry with her. Now as an adult in analysis, she would relapse into this non-stop compulsive activity when Kohut would go on vacation. He realized that her need state was in finding, now losing, an essential companion, her analyst, that lay behind her pathology.

An essential likeness takes hold

And now Jonathan was talking.

He'd blurt things out. "Stupid!," "Barber!" "He's not the one!" "Stupid" was the stupid people he believed talked to him.

"Barber" was associated with a memory of the first time he went to get a haircut at three. His mother was there. He cried the whole time his hair was being cut. To Jonathan, it gradually became clear that the verbal ejaculation of "Barber" or "Barbara" was an indication that he was feeling anxious.

"He's not the one" was also explored. It was difficult for Jonathan to describe what this was about, but little by little, Jonathan realized that it was a way of saying that this person or that person was not the single most important influence of all the hundreds of people who talked to him. Finding an important influence came to the foreground.

For this was one of the central problems. Jonathan had been searching, in vain, for twenty-five years. Not only had he concretized impulses and feelings and ideas as voices, but to his mind they were the voices of real people who spoke to him. It was as if Jonathan was watching movies, immersed in productions he didn't realize he had created.

Here was the second central issue. Jonathan was a passive observer. The people talked. They fought things out and discussed things and put each other down. Groups of people would ally with each other and battle against each other in a conflict of different ideas and attitudes. But as far as Jonathan was concerned, these were different people sorting it out; Jonathan was observing.

It became clear that Jonathan wasn't involved in or organizing these various believed in people. He quietly and passively stood by, as hoards of people carried on to whatever extent that they did. For twenty-five years, he had been a passive observer within his own mind, believing that he was surrounded by hundreds of relatives and friends and famous people, some long dead. All were actively propounding their views; Jonathan had essentially ceased existing as a person; he had been colonized by the contents of his psyche.

Each voice was a person to him. With so much busyness around him, he had no difficulty being constantly entertained by the myriad beings around him. The loneliness that most isolated and reclusive people feel didn't exist for him. As mentioned earlier in the discussion of the vertical split, Dan Stern's ideas (1985) about the development of "self agency" are pertinent for Jonathan. He had lost the "volition" part of the volition–proprioception–felt consequences of actions sequence. In terms of being active and passive, he was only passive. He was absent an ability to direct himself. It didn't occur to him to enter in and try to make sense of the voices, of what each meant and what each represented. As far as he was concerned, these were actual people sorting ideas and attitudes out for him.

Dr. Steinmann tried antipsychotic medications on him, all the while trying to get him to understand that these voices were his own creation and most likely represented something from him or about him. Jonathan was surprised at such an idea, but gradually could see that each made sense. Having understood his exclamation of "Barber," he could see that there might be some meaning to each and every one of them.

He developed severe tachycardia on Zyprexa, Risperdal, and Seroquel. Finally, over a period of several months, he was able to tolerate 15 mg of Abilify. Yet, the voices were no less insistent and he still seemed preoccupied, but at least he was taking something. Due to a medication induced cardiac conduction defect, Abilify had to be lowered to 2 mg. He stayed on Abilify 2 mg for about a year before discontinuing it against medical advice.

During the next two years of intensive psychotherapy, he cleared tremendously, as doctor and patient came to grips with his voices, his retreats from reality, his abdication of his self to voices. Many sessions were spent in fascinating philosophical, religious, and spiritual conversations about the nature of reality and the meaning of life. Here was the deepening of an "alikeness" experience with Dr. Steinman.

The alter ego

Doris Brothers (1993) in her paper "The search for the hidden self: A fresh look at alter ego transferences" comments:

> When asked "What is a friend?" Zeno, the Greek philosopher (ca362-ca264BC), is reported to have given the somewhat cryptic reply "Another I" (or in Latin, "alter ego"). (Brothers, 1993, p. 191)

Brothers interprets "alter ego," as does one dictionary definition, as "another side of oneself, a second self." Gorney (1988), also exploring the details of the twinship transference, posited a "mutative sequence" wherein patients expressing this need for essential likeness become vitalized and develop the capacity for pleasure. In psychosis, what one finds is that the "alter ego" allows for a beginning sense of "wholeness" and that "wholeness" inside can be reflected by an experience of rejoining a real world of human being where affiliation can take place.

Jonathan finds "another I"

After two years, Jonathan is able to drive, goes to classes, has become computer literate and pursues a number of interests in the everyday world. He has driven with his girlfriend on long cross-country drives.

He comes punctually to sessions by himself. Most of the time he is not preoccupied by voices.

Sometimes, Dr. Steinman notices that he still does withdraw to his internal world of voices and preoccupations. This is generally when he's bored or doesn't know what else to do. This withdrawal of "cathexis," of psychic energy, has become a focus of his treatment. Whether habitual or due to upsetting life circumstances, these withdrawals to psychotic thinking are explored and understood over a number of sessions, just as a dream or a neurotic difficulty would be explored in a better put together patient.

At this point, he has friends, interests and is able to maintain a conversation most days for the full session. When he doesn't, this is the subject of enquiry. Where has he gone? What led to it? Is something upsetting him?

Here's a simple example. When he first came in, his mother would complain that he never washed and that he slept in his clothes for weeks at a time. Both he and his clothes had an odor. As this was explored, he initially would say nothing, but gradually elaborated ideas that clothing and bathing were surface phenomena. He was a deep man, unconcerned about such superficial things. Should he bathe or change his clothes, he'd be getting away from the voices and his spiritual pursuits.

As he talked about bathing and it's meaning to him, he started to shower regularly and changed his clothes. Not surprisingly, the body odor dissipated. Surprisingly, he had his hair and beard cut and trimmed on numerous occasions. He tells Dr. Steinman that his barber is a very pretty and engaging woman with whom he loves to chat. One can feel the "anti-isolation" at work.

Here's another example. Twenty-five years ago he had the experience of a shaft of light shattering through his body and shooting out through his chest; following this he felt very frightened, and then began to experience the beginning of the voices. Dr. Steinman wondered if this could have been a variation of Kundalini rising, an explosion of psychic energy unharnessed.

Dr. Steinman had seen a number of people who have talked about it and it's unsettling consequences after a period of intense meditation. This kind of intense appreciation and "de-pathologizing" of Jonathan's experience was, no doubt, an integral part of the depth of the twinship experience.

Jonathan told Doctor Steinman that there was a white cylinder of light hovering perpendicular to his head. Conscious of the possibility of the return of Kundalini—at least in his metaphor and the mystical and esoteric tradition—Steinman asked him about what happened to the cylinder. Slowly, it entered Jonathan's head from the top, gradually and slowly coursed down his spine into his pelvis. From there, energy streamed throughout his legs and body. This kind of bodily "re-cohering" or to use Gorney's terms "vitalization" are not uncommon as psychotic patients recover.

Dr. Steinman felt this was a good sign; "perhaps Kundalini, his psychic energy which had shot outside of himself twenty-five years ago had returned to him." Where he had previously had the contents of his psyche outside of himself in the form of voices, telepathy, and believed in people, the contents of his psyche and his psychic energy had returned to him, all his and under his control.

Jonathan beamed.

Crisis: a serious setback

As Jonathan improved, he and a friend drove a very long distance to a religious retreat. Jonathan stopped all medication in order to follow his spiritual practices. But, Jonathan had his own path of spirituality. Rather than pursuing his spiritual practice bit by bit, Jonathan became a spiritual warrior, spending fifteen or so hours per day immersed in his notion of the godhead.

Unsurprisingly, he snapped, becoming too disturbed for the spiritual compatriots; they called his family who flew out to get him and return him home. Now he was again withdrawn and seemingly catatonic. He spoke little, ate and drank little and withdrew into a world of inwardness. He looked psychotic but I sensed that he was immersed in the self in the tradition of the Hindu mystics.

> Dr. Steinman recounts:
> "I talked to his family and him—as best he could understand—about the dangers of what he was doing and told them that the hospital might be the best place for him. They would have none of it. So the retreat continued, He became too weak to come to my office, so I visited him at home, talking about his retreat inwardly and what psychological and spiritual mechanisms might be going on. He stayed fixed in his inward gaze."

After some time of his not speaking and with little nutrition entering his body, perhaps three months, I prevailed upon his family to take him to the emergency room. They refused to call the police and brought him there themselves. He required five liters of fluid. I pushed for him to go into the hospital, but he spoke and told me he would eat and drink and talk with me in the office and take antipsychotic medication.

Once home, he refused to do any of these things, again immersing himself in the blissful union of Brahmin with Atman, personal self with the great ocean of self. After several more months of the situation becoming even more dire, and refusing any nutrition or medication, I again convinced the family to bring him to the hospital. This time, six liters of fluid were required.

He continued catatonic looking, eyes rolled up into their sockets, meditating on the self. This time he refused to speak and take medication; other than intravenous nutrition, he refused anything to eat or drink. He was hospitalized on the psychiatry unit.

I hadn't hospitalized anyone on this particular psychiatry unit in a decade. When I came in to see Jonathan, I was told that I could talk to him, but there was now a hospitalist, an alleged specialist, who treated only hospitalized patients and would manage Jonathan. I didn't mind since I had often worked with residents and knew we would have a collegial interaction.

But the hospitalist was different. His mind was quickly made up, when Jonathan refused to speak with him. Jonathan was given IM antipsychotics, but to no avail. Two other specialists came in to evaluate him for ECT, electroshock treatment. When I raised a fuss about this plan, the hospitalist rather dismissively told me that this was the accepted treatment for catatonic schizophrenia. When I told the hospitalist that Jonathan was going through a spiritual experience, that would have led people to gather around him and throw garlands of flowers at him in India, he looked at me incredulously and reiterated that ECT was the treatment of choice.

I called everyone I knew in a position of power in the hospital to try to get the impending ECT put off or stopped altogether. My entreaties fell on deaf ears. With only a weekend separating Jonathan from ECT, I hit upon an idea that was worth a try.

Even though Jonathan seemed beyond contact to every else and hadn't uttered a word in months, refusing all oral nutrition,

I figured I would just spell out to Jonathan what was about to happen. I always assumed he could come out of this if he wanted to—or had to.

"Jonathan. You've taken this about as far as you can." I said softly and clearly to him while he seemed totally oblivious to anything but his inner preoccupations.

"If you don't start eating and drinking and talking to the staff in the next little bit, the doctors here will give you shock treatment. They'll put electrodes on your head and push a lever to try to shock you out of what they're calling catatonic schizophrenia. They're not listening to me when I tell them you're going through a spiritual experience of your own volition."

It took about three minutes for Jonathan to slowly say. "I understand." It took another fifteen minutes for him to take some water from me and perhaps twenty minutes for him to start to take some food from a staff member and slowly chew it. A few minutes later he began to talk to the staff member. Since the staff member was sympathetic to my approach of trying to talk with Jonathan, rather than shocking him out of his catatonia, she agreed to chart all of this so that the hospitalist would no longer have a case for giving Jonathan ECT.

Several days later, Jonathan was discharged on high doses of antipsychotics. Over the intervening time, Jonathan has gone totally off all antipsychotics; the antipsychotics had altered his heart rhythm on EKG, so we were able to slowly titrate down the antipsychotics with no ill effects. He became more involved in the world, exercising, taking classes, driving, shopping, gardening, and talking with family and friends. He became quite voluble with me about the meaning of his spiritual experience. An inner teaching went on for all his voices, as they fused into one person and his creations, not into voices coming from others.

Disruption and repair

As noted earlier in this book, one of the interesting ideas about how self psychology works is via Ernest Wolf's (1988) ideas about "disruption and repair." Within the context of a cohering selfobject experience—in this instance, a twinship one—setbacks are inevitable. What was going on in the transference/countertransference matrix was not completely clear but, once again Jonathan ventured out on his own into a solipsistic seeking journey, and once again, he became horribly lost.

However, with Dr. Steinman at his side, believing in him and remaining steadfastly available, Jonathan was able to reach out and make contact as Dr. Steinman stayed with him. Here was the "repair." The "alter ego" experience was re-established. What do these experiences of "disruption and repair" provide from the vantage point of the patient?

Hope is a key word in experiences of "disruption and repair." Here the patient can experience hope and an emerging self-confidence that things can go extremely wrong and, yet, vital and helpful connections can help "right" the ship. Jonathan got back on track.

Twinning strengthens the self

Dr. Steinman notes:

"Jonathan is not totally out of the woods yet. He sometimes spends a long time in meditation, which could mean that he is still preoccupied with voices; he denies it though, saying he is involved in a blissful union with the godhead. He definitely does understand now that voices are his own creations and definitely not actual beings clustered around him, speaking telepathically to him.

Jonathan's sense of agency is returning as he understands that he is the film director and the creator of any scenes in which he immerses himself. He is able to write and present his views of the nature of reality cogently. He has returned to studying different languages and has even been asked for advice and editorial comment on a friend's PhD thesis.

The control of his consciousness and where it goes is his task and responsibility. One way lies psychosis; one way lies spiritual pursuits; and another way lies dealing with the world in which most of us live. Jonathan is on his way to healing and reintegrating after a twenty-five-year psychosis."

CHAPTER EIGHT

Selfobjects in psychosis—the twinship compensation*

Concepts from psychoanalytic self psychology may be valuable in explaining confusing clinical experiences in psychotherapy with psychotic patients. In this article, we describe three clinical cases in which the patient believed that one of the therapist's body parts was actually the patient's. This body part "mixing up" has traditionally been understood in terms of part objects or transitional objects. We propose that the twinship selfobject experience provides a better understanding and guide to clinical intervention in these circumstances.

Introduction

Therapists who work with patients suffering from the psychoses often go through periods when they feel confused. Sometimes, particular kinds of confusion, such as when patients psychologically "borrow" body parts of their therapists, can be specifically identified; these confusions may have diagnostic or therapeutic implications.

---

*In honor of Dr. Marion Tolpin, Chapter Eight has been reproduced with permission from the American Journal of Psychotherapy. The citation is Garfield, DAS. & Tolpin, M. (1996). Selfobjects in psychosis. *American Journal of Psychotherapy*, 50: 2, 178–193.

For some time, psychodynamic psychiatrists have understood delusions, hallucinations, and bizarre behaviors as having a communicative function. Some authors (Garfield, 1987; Havens, 1986; Searles, 1979; Stolorow, Brandchaft, & Atwood, 1987; Sullivan, 1953) emphasize a "decoding" process that may be helpful in clarifying certain kinds of confusion. This represents a search for Shakespeare's time-honored "method to madness." Symbolization, dramatization, and thematic structuring are the common tools of this navigation.

Some experiences, however, defy even the sharpest conceptual tools. We believe that one such phenomenon is the patient's "borrowing" of the body or body parts of the therapist and this "borrowing" may be an essential aspect of the therapeutic situation. What may be required is not a "deciphering" of the symptomatology but rather, an understanding of what purpose or function the symptom serves for the patient. Here, Waelder's (1930) principle of the "multiple function" of symptomatology is in operation.

For example, we will describe a psychotic patient who asserts that "your leg is my leg" or another patient who, while pointing to the therapist's wrist, declares, "that is my wrist." The patient "mixes up" a body part of the analyst with her own body part. Most clinicians would describe this as a "merger" and consider it to be a sign of a patient prone to "primitive" experience. In some respects, this "body part borrowing" is the converse of a multiple personality. Here, the clinician is confronted with one mind (the patient's) in two separate bodies or body parts. This is similar to the "folie a deux" of the paranoid delusional dyad.

How is the function of such physical ownership to be understood? Is this simply a boundary merger or a breakdown in the demarcation of the self? Is the therapist serving as a type of "auxiliary ego" during a period of stress?

What are the transference implications of such communications? If it is a "merger" transference or therapeutic symbiosis of some kind, how are we to understand its specificity?

Perhaps newer notions from psychoanalytic self psychology may be of use in understanding the vicissitudes of working with psychotic patients. Herein comes the concept of the selfobject and the selfobject relationship. Once labeled as the "narcissistic neuroses" by Freud (1924) psychosis has evolved, psychoanalytically, through the traditional schools of conflict, ego, and object relations orientations. Insofar as narcissism and very basic deficits in self-cohesion, temporal continuity of the self, and positive affective coloring of the self are the essence of psychodynamic psychopathology in the psychoses, selfobjects may prove to be of utmost importance in the recovery process.

This article describes three cases where unusual body part "mixing up" occurred during psychotherapy. These phenomena have historical roots in the psychoanalytic concepts of "part-objects" and "transitional objects." It is our thesis that these body part possessions can also be seen as specific kinds of selfobject experiences evoked during times of empathic disruption in the therapeutic process. These instances can be looked at as a kind of twinship compensation. By compensation (Kohut, 1971) we mean that in the presence of partial developmental deficits, alternative sources of stabilization of the self may work to preserve cohesion. In these cases, having "one mind in two bodies (body parts)" serves to re-establish a vital source of cohesion for the patient. We also believe that this "mixing up" of body parts by the patient also takes place in neurotic patients, but, has its expression in unusual, but nonpsychotic, forms. This kind of restorative selfobject function may be a process that spans a wide range of psychopathology.

Case one: Claire's leg

Claire, a fifty-year-old woman, had been in and out of various community mental health treatment facilities before she settled into twice-weekly psychotherapy for the first time. She was an expressive and articulate woman and she carried with her a diagnosis of schizoaffective disorder. She had been divorced by her alcoholic husband after he had run off with another woman and she had returned to her home town. Her father, with whom she had had a lifelong conflictual and antagonistic relationship, was a prominent businessman in town and he had been willing, through a distantly controlled bank account, to pay for treatment for his now middle-aged, divorced daughter.

As a child, Claire reported, she had been a gifted artist. Even though her mother died when Claire was three years old, she recalled frequently sitting next to her mother, while her mother sculpted. Her mother would talk to her about the feel of clay and let her touch it. Claire was encouraged to draw and paint, and like her mother, she showed remarkable talent even as a child.

With her mother's death, Claire entered her father's custody. She had been shielded from his domineering personality by her mother, but now she was left exposed. He was rough and physically pulled her about when he wanted her to do something or be somewhere.

Although he soon remarried, Claire believed that he had intensely loved and felt rejected by his deceased wife. Insofar as Claire both looked like her mother and shared her mother's temperament and talent, her father, she felt, now resented her more than ever. Not only did Claire have to deal with her father's displaced punishment of his ex-wife, but she also had to deal with a stepmother who was jealous of the dead first wife. The stepmother resented having to raise the spitting image of her dead rival. Claire was frequently scolded by her stepmother and consequently, at every opportunity, Claire asked to go over to her grandparents house. Claire felt unconditionally loved and protected by her grandparents. Their love for, and enjoyment of her stood in stark contrast to her daily life with her father and stepmother.

The father, disenchanted with his new wife and resentful of his ex-wife and his daughter, began to drink heavily. It was during those times that he was cruelest. Claire recalls, that when she was five years old he lifted her up and told her to hold onto the top of the doorway molding. He promised her that he would support her but he let go and let her hang there. She remembers being terrified of falling and of spraining her left arm and shoulder trying to hold on.

Claire went on to Catholic boarding school where she was much happier. In her first year of college, she met her husband, Al, a businessman who adored her. He did well financially and they lived an affluent lifestyle.

When his business began to have trouble, he began to drink heavily and the couple argued. Claire insisted he get help and tried to help him herself. After their second daughter was out of high school, he divorced her and soon remarried.

Claire's life went downhill. She was hospitalized with a psychotic episode and soon thereafter, had uterine fibroids that required surgery and ultimately a hysterectomy. She was started on psychotropic medication and moved back to the town where her father and stepmother lived. She was dismayed that her father would not let her stay with them. She went on welfare and lived in a rooming house.

Treatment

In treatment, Claire was articulate in her description of her life history. She saw herself as having had a good amount of artistic talent but having had to sacrifice it to remedy the ailments of needy and defective men. In fact, she finished her college degree prior to entering therapy but majored, not in the fine arts, but rather, in social work.

As Claire came to feel understood by her psychiatrist, her life settled down. She obtained a job as a home health aide and moved into a small apartment. She was able to let art back into her life by visiting some of her favorite museums (which she had not done for several years) and even sketching a little bit. After eight months in treatment, Claire recalled her relationship with her mother in terms of working with clay-she recalled her mother's small but reassuring hands and the fun she felt when handling the wet clay. She also recalled the pain in her arm, shoulder, and neck which she experienced when her father hung her by her arms from the doorway.

Claire seemed to be very attentive to her male therapist. Initially, she placed him in an ideal category along with her male gynecologist who had helped her over her hysterectomy. She considered other men, like her father and her stepbrother, as evil. Yet, on many occasions, she was able to see how they had suffered from earlier deprivations. As the transference evolved, it had an idealized and romantic flavor. Claire would frequently tease her therapist about how lucky his wife must be and how, if she were a younger woman, she would chase after him. In many regards, it seemed that she wished to be the "apple of his eye." By being taken seriously and listened to carefully, she felt appreciated and her life outside of the therapeutic context settled down and moved forward.

In the middle part of the treatment, Claire was relaxed and playful with her dialogue. She began to ask "how's the leg?" and the therapist believed her to be teasing or joking. Was this a playful reference to a body part of a man she now trusted? Claire mentioned that the psychiatrist's secretary had said that he had had some back trouble. In fact, the therapist had moderately serious back problems and was intermittently limping. A week later, Claire asked "how's my leg?" while walking with the therapist from the waiting room into the office. This time, the therapist was confused about the reference, wondering if something was new or wrong with the patient's leg, Yet, she had, again, asked the question in the same casual and affectionate manner. As Claire's leg did not appear injured and she had not complained about it, the therapist asked what the reference to "my leg" meant. Claire simply laughed and told the therapist to stop being so silly. The patient made several references to "my leg" over the next two months in such a way to suggest that she intended to keep "whose leg it was" ambiguous. Although it was initially disorienting for the psychiatrist, he was able to tolerate the body part appropriation without any undue disruption in the treatment.

The "leg" references had a curious effect on the therapist. The countertransference reaction, at first, was one of a physical, psychological, and emotional "jolt." He wondered "exactly what is she doing to me and why does she need to do this to me?" Hypothesizing that his countertransference was "resonant" with Claire's healing state, the psychiatrist wondered with Claire if she were feeling that somehow, she was once again, being abused by a man about whom she felt strongly. She denied any such feelings.

Claire's life was progressing quite well at this point. Although she did not enter into any new relationships with men, she did renew some old acquaintances and she became more assertive about learning about her inheritance, which would be forthcoming at the time of her father's death.

She was doing quite well at her job and had been considered for promotion to supervisor.

It had not occurred to the psychiatrist that the difficulty he had been having with his back may have initiated this particular body part "mixing up." Was she afraid that an injury to "her man" might once again result in her being left hanging by her limbs in a precarious way? Did she fear a repetition in the transference of her loss of love from her father and husband? And was her effort to focus on the "leg" a way of making the therapist's health her necessary first priority? Perhaps, the shared "leg" served to keep her calm at this time in her treatment.

Part objects

A classical explanation of Claire's ambiguous reference to the therapist's leg would be that the "leg" served as a "part-object" representation; an attempt to internalize a symbol of a male "authority figure" with whom she could finally feel comfortable.

Freud (1900) introduced the concept of the part object in his exploration of an infant's earliest relations to need-satisfying objects. Claire's use of the therapist's leg would be seen as symbolic and based on this theory of sexual libido. Here, her unconscious desire to possess her father's power and sexuality takes form in the transference relationship via the primitive defense mechanism of incorporation.

Abraham (1924) took up Freud's treatise and expanded on the concept of the part object. Abraham saw an individual's relations to part objects as being one step on the path to full object love. With respect to psychosis, Abraham maintained that the melancholic and the paranoic manifested a narcissistic incorporation of either the whole object (the oral consumption of melancholia), or part of the object (the anal retention of the kleptomaniac or the paranoid patient). Thus, in Abraham's framework, one might view Claire's symptom as a response to her fear of losing the therapist. Thus, she incorporates a part of her loved object.

In working with psychotic children, Melanie Klein (1929) saw the psychotic reactions of children as being specifically configured by persecutory phantasy with the splitting of whole objects into part objects. The Kleinian (1935) part object view of Claire's leg would be that her internal representation of the therapist was split and the persecutory element was projected outward onto the therapist. "Now that he's hurt, he's dangerous." In a recapitulation of the earlier situation with the father, the patient attempts to neutralize the man's dangerous defects. Thus, she redoubles her efforts to both control him and make him "well" by taking on the burden of restoring the man to proper health. From this perspective, Claire can be seen to compulsively repeat her attempts to set the childhood situation right. The part object is used, in this model, defensively, prohibitively, and emotionally as Claire seeks to manage her competitive strivings in light of her overwhelming losses. The defense mechanism of distortion guides the perceptual "mixing up" of the part object and reaction formation characterizes her posture toward the external perpetrators of her misery.

Perhaps what is most clearly missing in an analysis of Claire's symptom from this point of view is the "context" within which the hypothesized "part object" relationship develops. For example, there was no sense of urgency in Claire's treatment during the time when this symptom appeared. Furthermore, her affect was calm; in some respects it was as if she and her psychiatrist "were in step with one another." This is where the concept of the part object has less explanatory power.

Case two: Steven's wrist

Another example of body part "mixing up" occurred in the treatment of Steven S., a twenty-three-year-old, single, Irish maintenance man who had been in and out of the hospital with a chronic non-affective psychosis. Steven grew up in an Irish part of Boston, the only child of an alcoholic bus driver father and a quiet, distant, and very religious mother. As a boy, Steven had some unpredictable and intense interactions with his mother's brothers, but, otherwise, was left to his own devices. The marriage between his parents grew strained. His father would stay away at night and an icy silence settled on the family interactions. Steven recalled waiting for his father. When Steven would come home from school, he would do schoolwork or play with trucks or watch baseball, but he was always keeping an eye or ear open for his dad to come home from work. His dad would come home less and less frequently. There was no discussion of this emptiness and loss in the household.

On occasion, Steven would emerge from his cocoon of introversion and get into fights in school. The principal would be called, his mother would have to come in and he would receive a ceremonial chiding from her about morals. Dutifully, he would walk home with her and behave himself for a period of time. The absence of his father made him more dejected. He remembered that both he and his dad were Red Sox fans and when he was very young, they had gone to a few baseball games. During his latency years, his dad had suggested that they go to a ballgame or two each year, but his dad would never follow up. One time, Steven pressured his dad to go and they set up a date on a Sunday afternoon, his dad never showed. This feeling-memory of waiting with no response embossed itself on Steven's psyche.

Treatment

Steven had been most recently hospitalized in July after the new residents had changed over at the training hospital. He had had his first psychotic episode some four years earlier after working for a year after high school.

The precipitant to that original hospitalization may have had to do with Steven's venturing to court a young woman, but neither the patient nor the charts were forthcoming with much information in that regard. The psychiatrist set up two forty minute appointments each week which were separate from team meetings, rounds, and other ward activities. The psychiatrist religiously adhered to the schedule but Steven rarely did. The patient was seldom on time to the clinician's office for the psychotherapy appointments, yet could always be found down the hall or in his room. When he was sought out by the psychiatrist, he would come into the session and stay for the full time. Steven would show up, unexpectedly, at lunchtime in the hospital cafeteria line when his psychiatrist was also going through the lunch line.

The patient had the delusion that he had been shot in the elbow at the Tomb of the Unknown Soldier when he was thirteen years old. He had been on a class trip down to Washington, D.C. and remembered the handsome, perfectly outfitted military guards at the National Cemetery. While the class filed by the tomb, he believed that one of the guards had inadvertently shot him in the elbow and that the bullet had traveled up his arm, across his chest, and down into his liver causing him to have cirrhosis. This was connected with a suicidal feeling, "suicidal cirrhosis." The experience of a "mixing up" of body parts came a week after the psychiatrist had returned from vacation. The patient spontaneously brought up a past interest in baseball, and commented that his wrist hurt him now and maybe something was broken. The therapist, somewhat concretely, asked if Steven's wrist was OK and if Steven had seen a doctor during the week that the therapist had been away. Steven did not respond and there was a long silence. At that point, the therapist offered that once during a high school football game, he had had a broken wrist. Pointing to the psychiatrist's wrist, Steven responded: "That's my wrist." When the psychiatrist questioned what Steven meant, the patient restated "that's my wrist." With some anxiety, Steven asked if the doctor wanted him to hold the injured wrist.

The countertransference effect on the psychiatrist was again of interest. The body part merger allusion made him anxious and he felt that he had "missed the boat." He was anxious that he would not be able to recapture the lost connection between the two of them. At the time, the psychiatrist also wondered if this was "homosexual" panic induced by the psychiatrist bringing his own body part into the discussion. The rest of the session was unremarkable. For the next two weeks, Steven asked about "the wrist" and, the psychiatrist was often unclear as to whose wrist he was referring. Perhaps this was an example of "joining hands together" in the therapeutic endeavor.

Here, one is again tempted to view the "wrist" as a part object symbolic of the patient's desire to be close to a transferential father figure. Yet, other theoretical possibilities emerge. To a certain extent, the shared body part could be viewed as a bridge between the patient and therapist; a "transitional space" or "transitional object" (Winnicott, 1953).

Transitional objects

Winnicott (1953) was the first to introduce the idea of the transitional object. It was a way station in the child's attempt to negotiate the needs of the internal world with the vicissitudes of the external environment:

> I have introduced the terms "transitional object" and "transitional phenomena" for designation of the intermediate area of experience, between the thumb and the teddy bear ... It is interesting to compare the transitional object concept with Melanie Klein's concept of the internal object. The transitional object is "not an internal object" (which is a mental concept)-it is a possession. Yet it is not (for the infant) an external object either. (Winnicott, 1953, pp. 230–237)

With respect to both Claire's leg and Steven's wrist, Waugh's (1962) paper on "The evocation of a proxy" is also instructive. He detailed how a patient may make use of an another person who is used to experience emotions, provide certain functions and conduct actions instead of the patient. This is close to Kohut's (1971) concept of a structural deficit. Waugh postulated that there was an insufficient dissolution of the earlier tie to the mother and that serious deficits in identity formation occur as a consequence.

In his discussion of the "therapeutic symbiosis," Searles (1979) posited something similar when he suggested that the patient and therapist must go through a stage of psychological merger in order for treatment to be effective. Searles also felt strongly that a crucial ingredient of therapy was the analyst's ability to allow the patient's natural inclination to heal the caregiver to operate. Thus, the patient must contribute to the healing of the analyst during the therapeutic symbiosis in order for the patient's treatment to be effective. Here, too, there is a merger symbiosis out of which the patient must re-individuate, similar to the evolving concept of the selfobject.

The problem with the transitional-object explanation for these clinical phenomena is that ongoing therapeutic relationships were already in place and that the clinical occurrences took place in the context of either trauma to the therapist's actual body (Claire's leg) or through lack of understanding of the patient's pain (Steven's wrist) during the time of the therapist's vacation.

This is where the concept of the selfobject may again, have more explanatory power.

Selfobjects

Given that in the treatment process there was playfulness and affection, Claire's leg provided her with a positive affective state, a sense of cohesion and a feeling of temporal continuity, it might be that this phenomenon functions as a "selfobject" for her. Here the therapist, which includes his body or body part, would be serving as psychological "glue" for an otherwise disintegrative self-experience. Steven's wrist, however, seemed to be different in this regard. The "mixing" of body parts was accompanied by a certain amount of anxiety. In retrospect, the anxiety might have been more in the therapist. Yet, the anxiety was not disabling and the session was able to continue. If the empathic failures were severe enough-the therapist's vacation and subsequent lack of attunement to Steven's emotional state during the vacation- the whole experience with the therapist, including the wrist selfobject, may have prevented much greater disintegration.

Kohut ideas about self-objects and self-object functions evolved and changed over time. In 1971, Kohut, began to define the self-object in terms of the patient's own experience.

> The small child, for example, invests other people with narcissistic cathexes and thus experiences them narcissistically, i.e., as self-objects. The expected control over such (self-object) others is then closer to the concept of the control which a grownup expects to have over his own body and mind than to the concept of the control which he expects to have over others. (Kohut, 1971, pp. 26–27)

Later, Kohut dropped the hyphen in the spelling of selfobject and thus emphasized the subjective, unifying role for the self that selfobjects play in human experience. He particularly emphasized the functional aspect of the selfobject as a substitute for the missing or defective self-esteem-regulating psychic structure. Stolorow and Lachmann (1980) followed Kohut's lead and noted that self-esteem-regulating structure "provides positive affective coloring of the self representation and also maintains the cohesion and stability of the self representation (the structural foundation upon which self-esteem rests)" (Stolorow & Lachmann, 1980, pp. 20–21).

In their illustrative article on the treatment of psychotic states, Stolorow, Brandchaft and Atwood (1987, pp. 132–172) describe a self-psychological approach to Anna, a young woman, who suffers from frequent dissolution of her sense of self. Validation of her subjective psychic reality is the prescribed cornerstone of the recovery process from psychosis. They asserted that what the patient required, early on, was for her analytst to "merge" with her during her shifting periods of feeling like she existed and like she didn't exist. It was only when the therapist could "decenter" himself from his own need to have the patient be a certain way, that the healing process could begin. This process, they proposed, entails the re-establishment of an archaic selfobject bond between patient and doctor-one which allows for a firming of the self. In this way, the patient can regain the experience of self in temporal continuity, affective aliveness, and internal cohesiveness.

McDougall (1989) described phenomena of "One body for two" in a chapter by the same title in her book *Theaters of the Body*. Her patient Georgette suffered from ulcers, and multiple psychosomatic dermatologic problems.

McDougall writes of an incident where she, the analyst, returned from vacation,

> "visibly sunburned" ... Georgette was clearly distraught about the analyst's appearance and could not speak but finally whispered, "My face is hurting so badly." We were able to understand that, apart from the conviction that my face belonged to her, she also felt guilty beyond words, because in some way my burnt visage was her fault ... In all her dreams and fantasies around this time it became manifest that not only did we share the same face but there also was only one body for the two of us. (McDougall, 1989, pp. 150–151)

McDougall calls this a "transference osmosis" and goes on to note that with each upcoming vacation break, Georgette's skin would erupt furiously in eczema. McDougall concluded: Her burning skin gave her a feeling of being alive, of being held together, while at the same time recalling the memory of an outer object (the analyst and their "shared skin") that was reassuring to her.

Breakdown of idealized figures: the twinship compensation

The cases above may be viewed in light of what Kohut (1977) and, more recently, in an unpublished manuscript, Lebovitz (1996, personal communication) refer to, as the twinship selfobject experience. By sharing common features with the analyst, patients are provided with a kind of reassurance that offsets a lost or shattered feeling about themselves. Lebovitz reports on his work with a patient whose earlier attempts to idealize both father and stepfather were unsuccessful. During the analysis, Lebovitz describes how the patient grows a beard similar to the analyst's. Lebovitz comments on the healing, selfobject transference ramifications of this "identity." In the cases above, both Claire and Steven can be seen to have developed idealizing selfobject transferences to their therapist. The accident to Claire's therapist and the empathic failure on the part of Steven's therapist traumatized the idealization, leaving the patients in dire inner straits. The body part mixing up can thus be seen as a transient twinship compensation to keep the self intact. McDougall's case of Georgette fits this model as well. This twinship compensation can also be seen in the "neurotic" case that follows.

Body selfobjects in neurosis

Like McDougall, we see these body selfobject experiences as being a kind of transference. In psychosis, McDougall describes this as transference "osmosis," following Kohut, we would describe this as a transient "alikeness" or twinship transference. These "archaic selfobject bonds," may also be present in neurotic patients, but may manifest themselves in different nonpsychotic forms.

Case three: Jennifer's dream of a braid

Jennifer, a twenty-eight-year-old woman, has struggled during her life with feelings of emptiness, despair, and anger. She sought analytic treatment after two prior psychotherapy experiences that were of modest but definite help. She was the director of marketing for a successful, large, software company and she lived alone. Most of her relationships with men were disappointing and annoying to her. Occasionally, she wondered if she would be happier if she were gay. Although she had a few girlfriends, she had no one whom she would consider a "soulmate." Jennifer's childhood was remarkable in that she had a pleasant but unengaged relationship with her mother and a very intense close relationship with her father. She had wondered, as the only child, if her father had not really wanted a boy. She recalled that she was upset but not surprised to find that her father had a mistress. Her father was a quite successful businessman. When she was eight years old, she vividly remembers being excited about his taking her on a business trip to Florida with him. When they arrived she was dismayed to find a woman, his lover, was at the business meeting as well and in fact, was staying at the same hotel. One evening he asked Jennifer if she would be OK watching TV in the hotel room alone for an hour or so and she said that she would be fine. She suspected that he was going to meet that woman. Three hours later he had not returned. A certain sense of emptiness, mixed with anger and despair set in.

In her analysis, Jennifer recalled turning off the TV after about one hour and sitting at the desk in the room staring in the mirror. She went to the closet and pulled out a shirt of her father's and put it on. She went into the bathroom and returned to the desk with a pair of small scissors that he kept in his accessories bag. At the time, she had long blonde hair. While sitting at the desk, wearing his shirt, she cut her hair short. She then went back to the closet and found some cufflinks of his and pulled the sleeves up and put the cufflinks into the holes on the cuffs. She studied herself in the mirror. She remembers wondering if she looked like a boy. She fell asleep on her bed. Her father woke her in the morning-she wasn't sure when he had returned. She had been embarrassed and hid the cufflinks and told him she wanted short hair for Florida and asked him if he liked it. He said he did. He had been amused and pleased that she had wanted to sleep in his shirt.

Jennnifer's analysis

As Jennifer discussed her difficulties with men and women in terms of trusting that they could or wanted to be close to her, she displayed a similar ambivalence toward the analyst. She needed to deny that the analyst was important to her. Jennifer would frequently seek to determine if the analyst was a "cupcake" like her mother or would be engaging like her father. She seemed to fear both.

As the analyst interpreted Jennifer's wishes to have a "soulmate" relationship in the same way she once had with her father, Jennifer became more animated and started to engage friends and potential boyfriends in a deeper and more lively way. After the second year of treatment, the analyst had a sports accident where she broke her hip. One month of analysis had to be cancelled. Upon her return to treatment, Jennifer was very concerned about how the healing was going for the analyst. She said she could visualize the bone fragments knitting themselves back together. One week after the sessions resumed, Jennifer reported a dream. In the dream, there was a simple image of herself as an adult with short salt-and-pepper colored hair with a braided wig added on to it. As she described the braid, she outlined its shape in the air as she lay on the couch. It had a ball at one end by her head, then jutted out a few inches and then "knitted" down her back. Jennifer associated to her childhood when she had long blonde hair and wondered if the analyst's injury had reminded her of her mother's "weakness" when she was a little girl. She reported her enthusiasm about bringing the dream in for the two of them to discuss.

Body part selfobjects in Jennifer's dream

The dream of the braid may represent another form-variety of the body part twinship compensation we have described for psychotic patients during periods of traumatic disruption to an idealized selfobject. The analyst's lack of availability leaves Jennifer in the same vulnerable position that she was in with her father when he left her alone in the Florida hotel room. Analysts from the classical school might argue that the "braid" was phallic and represented an identification with her father and her belief that her father desired her to be a boy. In addition, it could be argued that she twisted herself into a regressive, phallic configuration as a way of gaining a weapon to defeat her father's lover. Thus the braid would be viewed as a "part object." Those in the object relations school might argue that the braid served as a transitional object between her and the therapist, the braid being a symbol of her new "woman-ness" and, in addition, of carrying a healed version of the analyst's femur, with her.

Yet, the dream occurred in the context of a serious rupture in the analyst-patient relationship. Just as the shirt, cufflinks, and short hair were an attempt to hold onto a sense of vitality, purpose, and cohesiveness she had secured in her loving relationship with her father, the braid now provides the same sense of aliveness for her in her relationship with her analyst.

Conclusion

Ernest Wolf (1988) has described the process through which clinical improvement occurs for nonpsychotic patients. First disruptions must be non-traumatic. Second, a crucial selfobject bond must be re-established. This is predicated on the patient retaining or recovering the ability to make use of the therapist selfobject function. A similar template may guide the recovery process in psychosis. First, the patient must go through a process of establishing a network of selfobject relationships which permit the patient to bear and integrate difficult affects. This is at the heart of Wolf's method. The operative word here is "enlistment." In his *Treating The Self* (1988), Wolf points to the process of recruiting new selfobjects in the patient's environment as being a signal of the patient's recovery. With psychotic patients, these are often idealizing selfobject experiences. Wolf also goes on to point out a variety of different kinds of selfobject relationship needs that commonly occur over the life course.

As noted above, the patient goes through a process of self-disruption and restoration in the context of the analyst-patient relationship. No analyst is perfectly empathic and inevitable disruptions occur such as illness, vacations, oversights, interruptions, and inadvertent injuries. By having fears generated and then relieved, the patient can experience a self that falls apart and comes back together in a safe place.

When trauma strikes a vulnerable idealizing selfobject relationship, it is crucial that the therapist be able to tolerate the patient's response to disruption; these are attempts to reconstitute himself or herself.

Recognizing a twinship body-merger compensation guides treatment.

Here the analyst will allow the compensation to take place in a non challenging way. The clinician will recognize the need for the patient to re-establish a disrupted bond through the twinship compensation. The prior trauma can be discussed openly in this light and the "primitive expression" will remit. By viewing these phenomena in a classical or object relations model, interpretations may accentuate the trauma or the phenomena may be regarded as simply a "normal" part of therapy and the current trauma to the relationship will never be addressed. Perhaps, these kinds of body part twinship compensations or (mixing up of body parts) occur more frequently in work with patients who are or have been psychotic. Yet, in a way, these kinds of "mergers" can be viewed as first steps; the therapist is enlisted in the process of acknowledging, bearing, and putting into perspective (Semrad, 1969) certain unbearable affects. The second part of the healing equation pertains to the context of the patient-analyst relationship. Empathic disruption and restoration wherein the twinship compensation remits is the roadmap for a more vital cohesive self.

The concept of selfobjects and selfobject relationships may prove to have significant clinical power for clinicians working not only with neurotic patients but with psychotic patients as well. Self-esteem and "narcissistic deficits" have long been thought to be psychological keystones in psychosis.

Thus, attention to selfobject relationships may open new avenues through which psychotic patients may progress toward meaningful clinical improvement.

Summary

Psychoanalysts and psychotherapists who work with psychotic patients often encounter unusual clinical phenomena. In this article, a certain kind of phenomena is described, wherein the patient refers to a body part of the therapist as being owned by the patient. This "body part borrowing" or "merger" can be explained by the classical and object relations schools in terms of part and transitional object concepts. These diagnostic formulations will then guide therapeutic intervention.

Newer concepts, from the psychoanalytic school of self psychology, particularly that of the twinship selfobject experience, provide for a more effective intervention in these complex clinical situations. Certain psychotic responses, in these cases, delusional misperceptions, can be viewed as the patient's attempt to stave off empathic rupture and fragmentation. "Body part borrowing" in the treatment setting thus serves as a twinship selfobject compensation; it attenuates the unbearable affects generated by empathic failure. In this article, we offered clinical vignettes to illustrate these processes in two patients with psychosis and one with neurosis. We then offered various suggestions for clinical intervention based on a selfobject understanding of these phenomena.

CHAPTER NINE

The widening scope of psychoanalysis: self psychology and psychosis

We hope we have illustrated, the principles and practices of self psychology in the intensive psychotherapy of psychosis, providing a useful way to conceptualize and implement how we work with patients suffering from schizophrenia and related psychotic disturbances. All of the patients presented in depth in this book have had previous diagnoses of schizophrenia, yet all gradually worked through difficult and painful problems that underlay their delusional or hallucinatory experiences.

Concepts such as the vertical split, cross modal empathic attunement, fear of re-traumatization, the "forward edge," disruption and repair all help the self psychology therapist address the various deficits patients have and need to work through during the course of psychoanalytic psychotherapy. The three sections of the book—mirroring, idealizing, and twinship, have, of course, framed the foundation of this approach. It is important to note that with these foundational understandings of self psychology, people who were previously viewed as hopelessly mired in a psychotic process have been able to recover and some have been able to eventually come off antipsychotic medication.

As clinicians, with the three selfobject transferences/experiences in mind, we have a guide to the kind of work possible with those so disturbed. We see how mirroring and idealizing transferences aided Judith, Rachel, and Lois in their respective journeys through and out of psychosis. We see how Jonathan via his twinship selfobject relatedness was able to leave psychosis to pursue his spiritual pursuits.

The self psychological attitude which we are advocating in the treatment of psychosis does several things. It explains to the clinician what occurs, giving him some breathing space during the inevitable crises of treatment. It allows the clinician to re-chart a course, taking into account disruptions in mirroring, idealizing, or twinship experiences. Furthermore, it describes the vicissitudes of treatment, alerting one to potential means of repair of long standing selfobject rends in the fabric of our patient's psyche. With such a knowledge of the dynamics of the psychotic patient's selfobject transferences, we are prepared for the worst as we hope for the best, as we engage in an intensive psychotherapy focusing on the relief from suffering and the gradual movement away from a psychotic orientation.

From neurosis to personality disorder to psychosis

For the most part, psychotherapists and psychoanalysts, like us, have come to the ideas of self psychology after having been schooled in theories of classical Freudian, object relations, interpersonal/relational or ego psychological theories. As many self psychologists have pointed out, until recently, patients who do not neatly fit into neurotic classification schemas were thought to be poor candidates for psychoanalysis or analytic therapy. Then Kohut (1971) made his initial observations of working with the narcissistic behavior and personality disorders. Of course, Freud himself was very interested in psychosis and a whole group of analysts (Arieti, 1955; Benedetti, 1987; Fromm-Reichmann, 1959; M. Klein, 1930; Searles, 1960; Semrad, 1969) splintered off from mainstream psychoanalytic ways of working to bring their insights to bear on those with hallucinations, delusions, and thought disorders.

A convergence

A remarkable convergence of discoveries from infant observation researchers (Gropnick & Astington, 1988; Meltzoff & Borton, 1979; Tronick et al., 1978) has opened the door for a better understanding of the infrastructure of empathy and the subjective experiences of others.

As mainstream psychoanalysis has shifted to better incorporate these new research findings, practitioners of self psychology find themselves at the doorstep of being able to reach out to and assist those afflicted with Freud's "narcissistic neuroses." Kohut's (1971) landmark *Analysis of the Self* has led modern psychoanalysis to this entryway to psychosis and a waiting group of patients and clinicians are eager to meet in this new widening scope of psychoanalytic treatment.

Epilogue and return

Here we revisit Elizabeth Barrett Browning's poetic summation of how self psychology cures psychosis: "I love you not only for what you are, but for what I am when I am with you" (Browning, 1890).

Before he died, Kohut (1984) assembled the materials for his last book entitled *How does Analysis Cure?* In it, he describes the fundamental, in depth, psychoanalytic ideas of "understanding and explaining" as the centerpiece of treatment. Add to that Dr. Marian Tolpin's extension of Kohut's original ideas to the engine of psychoanalytic cure—the transference and its forward edge manifestations—and, as we have shown, the most disturbed of patients are now afforded that same possibility of cure. These journeys into and through psychosis are often long and arduous, but, as we have demonstrated, full recoveries are possible. We believe that self psychology, in all of its vicissitudes, provides new tools for reaching this lofty, remarkable healing, and at times curative, goal.

We hope that our in depth intensive psychotherapy case examples, exegesis and analysis, from a self psychology orientation, will serve as a beacon to other practitioners and as a guide for what goes on in the intensive psychotherapeutic treatment of psychosis. With such an approach, we hope that these illustrations of a self psychological treatment of psychosis will aid other clinicians in helping to release long suffering psychotic patients from their confusion, hallucinations, and delusions.

Using self psychology concepts and practicing intensive psychotherapy, we can aim for not just recovery and healing, but the possibility of a cure from a previously debilitating psychosis.

David Garfield, Chicago
Ira Steinman, San Francisco

REFERENCES

Abraham, K. (1924). A short study of the development of the libido. In: *Selected Papers on Psychoanalysis* (pp. 418–501). London: Hogarth, 1948.

Abramovitz, S. (1995). Killing the needy self: women professionals and suicide. *Progress in Self Psychology, 11*: 177–188.

Arieti, S. (1955). *Interpretation of Schizophrenia.* New York: Basic Books.

Bacal, H. (1985). Optimal responsiveness and the therapeutic process. *Progress in Self Psychology, 1*: 202–227.

Barnes, M., & Berke, J. (1991). *Two Accounts of a Journey Through Madness.* London: Free Association.

Benedetti, G. (1987). *Psychotherapy of Schizophrenia.* New York: New York University Press.

Brandchaft, B. (2007). Systems of pathological accommodation and change in analysis. *Psychoanalysis Psychology, 24*: 667–687.

Brothers, D. (1993). The search for the hidden self: A fresh look at alter ego transferences. *Progress in Self Psychology, 9*: 191–207.

Browning, E. (1890). *The Poetical Works of Elizabeth Barrett Browning.* London: Smith, Elder and Co.

Bullard, D. M. (1939). Application of psychoanalytic psychiatry to the psychoses. *Psychoanalysis Review, 26*: 526–534.

Cooper, D. (Ed.). (2001). *Psychiatry and Anti-Psychiatry.* London: Routledge.

Eckstein, R., & Wallerstein, R. (1958). *The Teaching and Learning of Psychotherapy*. New York: Basic Books.

Ellenberger, H. (1970). *The Discovery of the Unconscious*. New York: Basic Books.

Frayn, D. H. (1996). Enactments; An evolving dyadic concept of acting out. *American Journal of Psychotherapy, 50*: 2, 194–207.

Freedman, D, X., & Dyrud, J. E. (Eds.). (1975). *American Handbook of Psychiatry V, 2nd Edition. Vol. 5: Treatment*. New York: Basic Books.

Freud, A. (1966). A short history of child analysis. *Psychoanalytic Study of the Child, 21*: 7–14.

Freud, S. (1900). The interpretation of dreams. *S. E., 5*. London: Hogarth.

Freud, S. (1914). Remembering, repeating and working through. *S. E., 12*: 145–156. London: Hogarth.

Freud, S. (1914a). On narcissism: An introduction. *S. E., 14*: 67–102. London: Hogarth.

Freud, S. (1915). Repression. *S. E., 14*: 141–158. London: Hogarth.

Freud, S. (1924). Neurosis and psychosis. *S. E., 19*: 147–154. London: Hogarth.

Freud, S. (1925). Negation. *S. E., 19*: 233–240. London: Hogarth.

Freud, S. (1927). Fetishism. *S. E., 21*: 147–158. London: Hogarth.

Freud, S. (1940a [1938]). An outline of psycho-analysis. *S. E., 23*: 144–207. London: Hogarth.

Fromm-Reichmann, F. (1950). *Principles of Intensive Psychotherapy*. Chicago: University of Chicago Press.

Fromm-Reichmann, F. (1959). *Psychoanalysis and Psychotherapy*. Chicago: University of Chicago Press.

Gabbard, G. (1994). *Psychodynamic Psychiatry in Clinical Practice*. Washington, DC: American Psychiatric Press.

Gallese, V. (2001). The "shared manifold" hypothesis. From mirror neurons to empathy. *Journal of Consciousness Studies, 8*: 33–50.

Garfield, D. (1987). Affect translation in the psychotherapy of psychosis: Semrad's approach revisited. *Psychotherapy, 24*: 381–386.

Garfield, D. (2001). The use of vitality affects in the coalescence of self in psychosis. *Progress in Self Psychology, 17*: 113–128.

Garfield, D. (2009). *Unbearable Affect: A Guide to the Psychotherapy of Psychosis*. London: Karnac.

Garfield, D. A. S., & Havens, L. (1991). Paranoid phenomena and pathological narcissism. *American Journal of Psychotherapy, XLV*: 160–172.

Garvey, C. (1977). *Play*. Cambridge, MA: Harvard University Press.

Goldberg, A. (1995). *The Problem of Perversion*. New Haven, CT: Yale University Press.

Goldberg, A. (1999). *Being of Two Minds*. Hillsdale, NJ: The Analytic Press.

Goldberg, A. (2001). *Errant Selves: A Casebook of Misbehavior*. Hillsdale, NJ: The Analytic Press.
Golomb, E. (1992). *Trapped in the Mirror*. New York: Quill, William Morrow.
Gorney, J. E. (1998). Twinship, Vitality, Pleasure. *Progress in Self Psychology, 14*: 85–106.
Greenberg, J. R., & Mitchell, S. A. (1983). *Object Relations in Psychoanalytic Theory*. Cambridge, Mass: Harvard University Press.
Gropnick, A., & Astington, J. W. (1988). Children's understanding of representational change and its relationship to the understanding of false-belief and the appearance of the illusion-reality distinction. *Child Development, 59*: 26–37.
Havens, L. L. (1986). *Making Contact*. Cambridge, MA: Harvard University Press.
Jacobs, T. (1986). On countertransference enactments. *Journal of the American Psychoanalytic Association, 34:* 289–302.
Jaspers, K. (1963). *General Psychopathology*. Manchester, England: Manchester University Press.
Klein, M. (1929). Personification in the play with children. *International Journal Psychoanalysis, 10*: 193–204.
Klein, M. (1930). The psychotherapy of the psychoses. *British Journal of Medical Psychology, 10*: 242–244.
Klein, M. (1935). A contribution to the psychogenesis of manic-depressive states. *International Journal Psychoanalysis, 16*: 145–174.
Klein, M. (1946). Notes on some schizoid mechanisms. In: *Envy and Gratitude and Other Works. 1946–1963* (pp. 176–236). New York: Delacorte, 1975.
Kohut, H. (1959). Introspection, empathy, and psychoanalysis—An examination of the relationship between mode of observation and theory. *Journal of the American Psychoanalytic Association, 7*: 459–483.
Kohut, H. (1960). Beyond the bounds of the basic rule—some recent contributions to applied psychoanalysis. *Journal of the American Psychoanalysis Association, 8*: 567–586.
Kohut, H. (1968). The psychoanalytic treatment of narcissistic personality disorders—outline of a systematic approach. *Psychoanaytic Study of the Child, 23*: 86–113.
Kohut, H. (1971). *The Analysis of the Self*. New York: International Universities Press.
Kohut, H. (1977). *Restoration of the Self*. New York: International Universities Press.
Kohut, H. (1984). *How Does Analysis Cure?* (A. Goldberg, & P. Stepansky, Eds). Chicago: University of Chicago Press.
Laing, R. D. (1961). *The Self and Others*. London: Tavistock.
Laing, R. D. (1962). *The Divided Self*. London: Pelican.

Laing, R. D., & Cooper, D. (1964). *Reason and Violence: A Decade of Sartre's Philosophy*. London: Tavistock.

Laing, R. D., & Esterson, A. (1964). *Sanity, Madness and the Family: Families of Schizophrenics*. New York: Penguin.

Lebovitz, P. (1996). Personal communication.

Libet, B., Freeman, A., & Sutherland, K. (2001). *The Volitional Brain: Toward a Neuroscience of Free Will*. Thorverton, UK: Imprint Press.

Litowitz, B. (1998). An expanded developmental line for negation: Rejection, refusal, denial. *Journal American Psychoanalytic Association, 46l: (1)* 121–148.

McDougall, J. (1989). *Theaters of the Body*. New York and London: W. W. Norton.

McLaughlin, J. (1987). The play of transference: some reflections on enactment in the psychoanalytic situation. *Journal of the American Psychoanalytic Association, 35*: 557–582.

Meltzoff, A. N., & Borton, W. (1979). Intermodal matching by human neonates. *Nature, 282*: 403–404.

National Academy of Sciences. (1969). *The Drug Efficacy Study of the National Research Council's Division of Medical Sciences, 1966–1969*. Washington: National Academy of Sciences.

Nemiah, J. C., & Sifneos, P. E. (1970). Psychosomatic illness: A problem in communication. *Psychotherapy and Psychosomatics, 18*: 154–160.

Ogden, T. H. (1986). *The Matrix of the Mind: Object Relations and the Psychoanalytic Dialogue*. Northvale, NJ: Jason Aronson.

Ombredance, A. (1951). *L'aplaise et l'elaboration de la pensee explicite*. Paris: Paris Presses, Universitaire de France.

Orange, D., Atwood, G., & Stolorow, R. (1997). *Working Intersubjectively: Contextualism in Psychoanalytic Practice*. Hillsdale, NJ: The Analytic Press.

Pao, P. -N. (1979). *Schizophrenic Disorders: Theory and Treatment from a Psychodynamic Point of View*. New York: International Universities Press.

Perls, F. S. (1992). *Ego, Hunger, and Aggression: A Revision of Freud's Theory and Method*. Gouldsboro, ME: Gestalt Journal Press.

Piaget, J. (1952). *The Origins of Intelligence in Children*. New York: W. W. Norton.

Racker, H. (1968). *Transference and Counter transference*. New York: International University Press.

Redlich, F. C., & Freedman, D. X. (1966). *Theory and Practice of Psychiatry*. New York: Basic Books.

Rosen, J. N. (1953). *Direct Analysis: Selected Papers*. New York: Grune & Stratton.

Searles, H. (1965). *Collected Papers on Schizophrenia and Related Subjects*. New York: International Universities Press.

Searles, H. (1979). Concerning therapeutic symbiosis: The patient as symbiotic therapist, the phase of ambivalent symbiosis, and the role of jealousy in the fragmented ego. In: *Countertransference* (pp. 172–192). New York: International Universities Press.
Semrad, E. (1969). *Teaching Psychotherapy of Psychotic Patients*. (D. Van Buskirk, Ed.). New York, NY: Grune and Stratton.
Shane, M. & Shane, E. (1993). Self psychology after Kohut: one theory or many. *Journal of the American Psychoanalysis Association, 41*: 777–792.
Sharpe, E. F. (1940). Psychophysical problems revealed in language: an examination of metaphor. *International Journal of Psycho-analysis, 21*: 201–213.
Sheets-Johnstone, M. (1998). *The Primacy of Movement*. Amsterdam: John Benjamins Publishing Companies.
Siegel, A. (1996). *Heinz Kohut and the Psychology of the Self*. London: Routledge.
Spence, S. A., & Frith, C. D. (1999). Towards a functional anatomy of volition. *Journal of Conscious Studies, 6*: 11–29.
Steinman, I. M. (2009). *Treating the "Untreatable": Healing in the Realms of Madness*. London: Karnac.
Stern, D. (1985). *The Interpersonal World of The Infant*. New York: Basic Books.
Stern, D. (2004). *The Present Moment in Psychotherapy and Everyday Life*. New York: W. W. Norton.
Stern, D. (2010). *Forms of Vitality: Exploring Dynamic Experience in Psychology and the Arts*. New York: Oxford University Press.
Stern, D. B., Mann, C. H., Kantor, S., & Sclesinger, G. (1995). *Origins: A Review of Pioneers of Interpersonal Psychoanalysis*. Hillsdale, NJ: The Analytic Press.
Stolorow, R. D. & Lachmann, F. M. (1980). *Psychoanalysis of Developmental Arrests*. New York: International Universities Press.
Stolorow, R., Brandschraft, B., & Atwood, G. (1987). *Psychoanalytic Treatment: An Intersubjective Approach*. Hillsdale, NJ: Analytic Press.
Stolorow, R. D. & Saccharides, D. (1987). Affects and selfobjects. In: R. D. Stolorow, B. Brandchaft, & G. E. Atwood (Eds.), *Psychoanalytic Treatment: An Intersubjective Approach* (pp. 66–88). Hillsdale, NJ: Analytic Press.
Stolorow, R. D., Brandchaft, B., & Atwood, G. E. (1987). The treatment of psychotic states. In: *Psychoanalytic Treatment: An Intersubjective Approach* (pp. 66–85). Hillsdale, NJ: The Analytic Press.
Stone, L. (1954). The widening scope of indications for psychoanalysis. *Journal of the American Psychoanalytic Association, 2*: 567–594.
Sullivan, H. S. (1953). *The Interpersonal Theory of Psychiatry*. New York: W. W. Norton.

Sullivan, H. S. (1956). *Clinical Studies in Psychiatry*. New York: W. W. Norton.
Sullivan, H. S. (1968). *The Interpersonal Theory of Psychiatry*. New York: Norton.
Tolpin, M. (1993). The unmirrored self, compensatory structure, and cure: The exemplary case of Anna O. *Annual of Psychoanalysis, 21*: 157–177.
Tolpin, M. (2002). Doing psychoanalysis of normal development: Forward edge transferences. *Progress in Self Psychology, 18*: 167–190.
Tolpin, P., & Tolpin, M. (1996). *Heinz Kohut: The Chicago Institute Lectures*. Hilldsdale, NJ: Anayltic Press.
Tronick, E., Als, H., Adamson, L., Wise, S., & Brazelton, W. B. (1978). The infant's response to entrapment between contradictory messages in face-to-face interaction. *Journal of Child Psychiatry, 17*: 1–13.
Vaillant, G. (1977). *Adaptation to Life*. Boston: Little and Brown.
Waelder, R. (1930). The principle of multiple function. *Psychoanalytic Quarterly, 15*: 45–52.
Wallerstein, R. S. (1986). *Forty-Two Lives in Treatment: A Study of Psychoanalysis and Psychotherapy*. New York: Guilford.
Waugh, M. (1962). The "evocation of a proxy": A psychological maneuver, its use as a defense, its purposes and genesis. *The Psychoanalytic Study of the Child, 17*: 451–469.
Werner, H. (1948). *The Comparative Development of Mental Development*. New York: International Universities Press.
Werner, H., & Kaplan, B. (1984). *Symbol Formation*. Hillsdale, NJ: Lawrence Erlbaum.
Westen, D. (1992). The cognitive self and the pychoanalytic self: Can we put ourselves together? *Psychological Inquiry, 3*: (1) 1–15.
Will, O. A. (1961). Process, psychotherapy, and schizophrenia. In: A. Burton, (Eds.), *Psychotherapy of the Psychoses* (pp. 10–42). New York: Basic Books.
Winnicott, D. W. (1953). Transitional objects and transitional phenomena—A study of the first "not me" possession. In: *Collected papers* (pp. 229–242). New York: Basic Books.
Winnicott, D. W. (1960). Ego distortion in terms of the true and false self. In: *The Maturational Processes and the Facilitating Environment* (pp. 140–153). New York: International Universities Press.
Wolf, E. (1988). *Treating the Self*. New York: Guilford.

INDEX

Abraham, K. 135
Abramovitz, S. 77
active self 75–76
Adamson, L. 148
affects 5–6
"alien hand syndrome" 73
Als, H. 148
"alter ego" 120, 122, 127
Analysis of the Self 60, 74, 101, 149
antipsychotic medications 57, 121
Arieti, S. 148
"associational psychology" 14
Astington, J. W. 148
Atwood, G. 69, 130
Atwood, G. E. 140
"authority figure" 134

Bacal, H. xxv, 39
Barnes, M. xviii
Being of Two Minds 32, 60
Benedetti, G. 148

Berke, J. xviii
bipolar affective disorder xxxi, 44, 70
bipolar self 22, 44–45
body's movements 64–66
Borton, W. 112, 148
Brandchaft, B. 130, 140
Brazelton, W. B. 148
Brothers, D. 122
Browning, E. 22, 149
Bullard, D. M. xix

case studies
    Claire 131–135, 138–139, 141
    Dr. Steinman 23, 87–89, 105–106
    Jane 61–68, 70, 73, 75–77
    Jennifer 141–144
    Jonathan 109–127, 148
    Judith 3–5, 12–14
    Rachel 81–95
    Steve 70–72, 75–77
    Steven 136–139, 141

coherence 43–44
convergence 148–149
Cooper, D. xvii
countertransference xxi, xxxv, 20–21,
    48, 62, 71, 127, 134, 137
  concordant 48, 62, 89
crisis 124–126
cross modal attunement xxxi,
    xxxiii–xxxv, 112, 147

"decoding" process 130
deficit 29–30, 100
delusion 11
  "authochthonus" 115
  defensive structure 101
  healing 105
  history 15–18
  ideas 100
  nature 99
  reality 104
disavowal 66
  unrecognized talents 61
disintegration 83–84
disruption 126–127
dramatization 130
Dyrud, J. E. xix

Eckstein, R. xix
ego psychology 9
Ellenberger, H. xxiii, 8, 14
empathic failure, the nature of 48
empathy 14, 54
engaging affects 82–83
enlistment xxviii, 89, 144
Errant Selves 32, 60
Esterson, A. xvii
Everyday Life 113
experiencing self 75–76

"feelings" 6
Forms of Vitality 113
fragmentation 118
Frayn, D. H. 65–66

Freedman, D. X. xviii
Freeman, A. 72
Freud, A. 114
Freud, S. xxiii, xxv–xxvi, 7, 9, 22, 60,
    65–66, 114, 130, 134
  psychosexual developmental
    schema 22
Frith, C. D. 73
Fromm-Reichmann, F. xix, 148

Gabbard, G. 66
Gallese, V. 7
Garfield, D. xxv, xxxi–xxxii,
    xxxiv–xxxv, 32, 101, 130
Garfield, D. A. S. xxxiv, 101
Garvey, C. 114
Goldberg, A. 32, 60, 69–70, 74, 90
Golden Gate Bridge 41, 43, 81, 86
Golomb, E. xxxiii
"Good Angel" 14, 18
Gorney, J. E. 122, 124
grandiosity xxvii, 22
Greenberg, J. R. 69
Gropnick, A. 148

hallucinations 11
  history 15–18
Havens, L. xxxiv, 101
Havens, L. L. 130
How does Analysis Cure 120, 149

interpretation 54
The Interpersonal World of the Infant
    xxxiii, 72

Jacobs, T. 65
Jaspers, K. 99, 100, 153

Klein, M. xx, 66, 138, 148
Kohut, H. xxii, xxvi, xxxi–xxxii, xxxv,
    21, 24, 54, 59–60, 69, 77,
    98, 101–103, 105, 120, 131,
    138–139, 141, 148–149